"What a feast! Dr. Julia
table for us with this ric
munity and thirst for belonging. She plays the cook, the server, the
host, and the co-participant in this written meal for our souls. Her
words, and the life she lives, will encourage your heart and mind.
Please follow her lead and nourish both your body and community by incarnating these truths."

—MATT DYMENT
Wilderness instructor

"In *Transcendence at the Table*, Dr. Julia Hurlow masterfully
champions a trinitarian theology of the table marked by love and
belonging. With clarity and conviction, she holds space for each of
us to reclaim a sense of the Imago Dei in ourselves and others. This
book is a profound call to be about the deeper work of unity and
not mere uniformity."

—DREW MOSER
Author of *The Enneagram of Discernment:
The Way of Vocation, Wisdom, and Practice*

"For Julia, what happens at the table is not a theory but a lifestyle.
I've observed firsthand how she pursues the life of presence she describes, where the table is wide and full of grace. This book is an invitation into a sacred space where we can discover more of God in
and through each other. May we lean in and heed the call to return
to the table, a place of hope and healing, beauty, and belonging."

—SARAH E. WESTFALL
Writer and host of the *Not My Story* podcast

"Dr. Hurlow's work is a prophetic and much-needed call back into the transformative realities of community and intimate connection that are fostered when life is lived around the table. In some ways Dr. Hurlow calls the church back to its roots as a community of believers, and yet she also calls us to anticipate the fullness of redemption when salvation is celebrated at the feast of the Lamb. Dr. Hurlow extends a powerful and much-needed invitation to step into a distinctly Christian way of living and being in the world, an identity that is embodied in life together at the table. So much of the brokenness experienced in the world today can be opened to redemption if we take Dr. Hurlow's call seriously to gather at the table in mutual relationship, to answer the invitation to unity and oneness in the name of God, Jesus, and Spirit. Put simply, Dr. Hurlow's work here is a vital and much-needed voice in our cultural climate today."

—**AARON CLOUD**
Pastor of Ministry Development
GracePoint Wesleyan Church

"In a time when there has been a significant decline in the familial and communal identity around the table, Julia has a way of helping us reimagine with a new sense of appreciation, as we understand and recapture the value of the table once again, not only just a place where bread is broken, good food shared, stories told, a friendship built, but above all, the table is an altar, designed by God. Julia challenges us to have a renewed sense of wonder for that table, the extension of grace through the power of the Holy Spirit."

—**SAMUEL KEFAS SARPIYA**
Executive Director of the Center
for Nonviolence and Conflict Transformation

"Julia offers a journey to explore the profound life-giving transformation that occurs when we gather around a table. In this work, we get a deep, beautiful imagery and a robust biblical narrative that give a framework for a lifelong exploration and participation in the table. Our own life experience of actual gatherings around Julia's table and the reshaping of our own hearts stand as a testament to the life-giving truth of these stories and values. As you dive into this work, you will find yourself reflecting on your own encounters at the table and be provoked with a longing to experience more."

—TYLER AND KRISTIN GREEN
Community Catalyst for Hobby Lobby Ministry Investments
and stay-at-home mother, respectively

"In a dramatic narrative Hurlow presents the lost art to *know* and to be *known* . . . May we find the courage to come to the table not as our manicured selves but as the selves we are now, so our sense of self, our identity, and our belonging can be restored as intended by God."

—ESTHER JADHAV
Assistant Vice President of Intercultural Affairs, Asbury University

"As a wise and gifted scholar and practitioner, Dr. Hurlow embodies the meaning of the table throughout her life—not only in her education and work, but in her relationships and daily practices as well—making her uniquely qualified to write *Transcendence at the Table*. Julia beautifully weaves her personal experiences and stories into the larger narrative of the table. The theological foundations of *Transcendence at the Table* are meaningfully complemented by the philosophical and practical reflective questions included throughout the book. With care, Julia provides advice and challenges readers to engage in and embody the table in their own lives, inspiring readers to contemplate the sacred practice of welcoming others to their own tables."

—KELLY A. YORDY
Assistant Professor of Higher Education, Taylor University

"With this rich work, Julia recovers the image, purpose, and hope of community—the table. She prepares readers with a plate of goodness and invites us to sit together, to commune together, to share stories together, all around the table. She provides a vibrant history of communion and table and gathering while sharing personal stories and intentional reflection. Crack this book open, gather a few friends, and find belonging—I cannot recommend this book more."

—SARAH JOBSON
Wife, mom, leadership coach, and mentor

"Dr. Hurlow recaptures the essence of breaking bread and frames it as a spiritual practice vital to our identity as followers of Jesus and members of the human race. . . . Whether those invited to our table have backgrounds, or are strangers, the intention of the table is to include others. We all have a need to belong. The gathering of people at a table brings that need to the center and invites others in. . . . Dr. Hurlow sets a table before us with all that we need to feast upon the imagery and the understanding of our loving Father's desire for his beloved children."

—JERE WITHERSPOON
Mother of three, long-time resident of western Oregon

Transcendence at the Table

Transcendence at the Table

A Transfigurational Experience
While Breaking Bread Together

Julia Hurlow

Foreword by Leonard Sweet

WIPF & STOCK · Eugene, Oregon

Wipf & Stock
An Imprint of Wipf and Stock Publishers
199 W. 8th Ave., Suite 3
Eugene, OR 97401

www.wipfandstock.com

PAPERBACK ISBN: 978-1-7252-6680-3
HARDCOVER ISBN: 978-1-7252-6681-0
EBOOK ISBN: 978-1-7252-6682-7

Manufactured in the U.S.A.   11/16/20

To those who have created a space for each person
on Thanksgiving in your Walhalla home.
. . . you have shown me the redemption
of sharing the Larger story, around the table!

To those who have come, participated, and
communicated around the table, it has been sacred.
. . . it has been quite an experience to share times of listening,
grieving, and celebrating together!

To those who have still yet to come join us at the table . . .
may this table always have room to pull up another chair
with your nametag awaiting!

May this universal place of gathering offer equity and be unending
in its ability to offer unification for all who come.

May there be an expansive imagination for how intentionality can
set spaces of inclusivity by offering invitation to all,
to come, and to have a seat.

May the particularities of each personality
who are present, participate freely.

May there be communication smothered in compassion,
seasoned with conflict, and garnished with celebration.

May the transparency of each person present
be enhanced by breaking bread together
through the transcendence that comes at the table.

Contents

Foreword

A REVEALING RABBINIC STORY captures what happened after the destruction of the temple in 70 AD and the subsequent disappearance of the locus and focus of Jewish faith, the priestly class and sacrificial cult.

> One day, Rabbi Yohanan ben Zakkai was going from Jerusalem in the company of Rabbi Jehoshua when he saw the sanctuary [of the Temple] in ruins. "What a calamity for us," exclaimed Rabbi Jehoshua, "that this place where expiation was made for the sins of Israel lies in ruins!" Rabbi Yohanan said to him: "My son, do not be sad! We have a means of expiation that is equivalent, it is the practice of goodness according to what is written: 'what I want is love, not sacrifice'" (Hosea 6:6).[1]

The rabbis (collectively known as the "Sages of Blessed Memory") and the architects of the Mishna and the Talmud rebooted Judaism not around the temple but around the table. Two tables, to be exact. The table in the synagogue at which the sacred Scriptures were read, and the table in the home where food was served to multiple generations. The table is what replaced the temple in the liturgical life of Judaism.

Where priests presided at an altar, the rabbis (not a vocation found in the Hebrew Bible) presided at a table. Every synagogue

---

1. As found in *Avot de-Rabbi Nathan*, 11a, a homiletical exposition (compiled between 700–900 CE) of the Mishnaic tractate *Pirkei Avot* (Ethics of the Fathers).

must have an ark, where the Torah scrolls are kept. Every synagogue must have a table, from which the scrolls are read. Other than that, synagogues are free to take the architectural form of the communities where they are located. The original idea was for the synagogue to be the tallest building in town, but Jews learned to keep their heads down and not stick their architectural necks above others.

Parents presided at the table in the home where everyone studied, prayed, and ate together. One of the most sacred Jewish holidays, Passover (Pesach), is not celebrated in the synagogue at all. Only around the home table presided over by the father and mother who lead the liturgy (Haggadah or "narration") recounting God's liberation of Israel from slavery and God's continued presence in the lives of the people. The liturgy starts with the youngest member of the family posing four questions about the story which are answered during the extended meal.

Christians reframed the animal sacrifices offered at the temple to be the life sacrifices offered at the synagogue and home. "Sacrifice" comes from the words *sacer* (sacred) and *facere* (make). To "sacrifice" something is to make it sacred. What Christians did was to make sacred their whole life. They made everything they did, and everything they were, sacred. All of life became holy and a "living sacrifice" (Romans 12:1). You no longer sacrificed an animal to make your offering sacred. You made your whole life sacred.

At the very beginning of Christianity, the temple and table were both central. Believers met in the temple for worship, where the priests chanted psalms and sacrificed animals. But they met at home to celebrate the liturgy of the table.

Day by day, as they spent much time together in the temple, they broke bread at home and ate their food with glad and generous hearts (Acts 2:46).

The first Christians did not come together primarily to worship but to eat a sumptuous meal together. "They devoted themselves to the apostles' teaching and to fellowship, to the breaking of bread and to prayer" (Acts 2:42). They came together to experience the joy of eating the Lord's Supper on the Lord's Day, and while eating there was grand fellowship bathed in prayer. The teaching could take place before the meal, after the meal, or even sometimes during the meal. In Greek the breaking of bread/fellowship (no "and") are simultaneous activities. So their "devotion" was to three things: fellowship around meals, prayer, and apostles' teaching. The German theologian and Near Eastern scholar Joachim Jeremias (1900–1979) argued that the core Eucharistic concept of anamnesis ("Do this in memory of me") is given as a reminder for God more than a remembrance for us. Like the rainbow, which is a reminder not to us but to God not to flood the earth, the Eucharist was a reminder to Jesus to return to the earth and join us at the Messianic Table.

Dr. Julia Hurlow has written a captivating study of the importance of the table, as she summons us to come back to the table. She shows how meals in real life, like meals in the Bible, should never be approached as mere physical fulfillment. They are times of social significance, theological meaning, and spiritual sustenance. Meals can be times of covenant-making, or covenant-breaking. They are that important.

This book is that important. I came away from it more resolved than ever to stop labeling, and start tabling. Instead of labeling people based on difference and monochromatic bias, let's start tabling difference and polychromatic uniqueness around food and conversation, listening, and learning. "Table It" is not a bureaucratic procedure out of St. Roberts' Rules of Order, but a liturgy produced straight out of St. Paul's Rules of the Spirit.

Here is a book that helps us learn from our Jewish neighbors the biblical meaning of "Tabling" and the directive "Table It."

Leonard Sweet
Professor at Portland Seminary, Drew University,
Evangelical Seminary, and Tabor College
Best-selling author (*Rings of Fire*)
Founder of PreachTheStory.com

Acknowledgments

RAISING A GLASS TO so many . . . present, near and far! Tables have been a grounding place in my life, curiosity and imagination have been embodied in so many of my companions around a shared meal. If my kitchen had a theme song, it would be "Born" by Over the Rhine; "Put your elbows on the table . . . I'll listen long as I am able . . . There's nowhere I'd rather be."

As this compilation of writings came together it was from a plethora of shared meals, participating in the Eucharist, researching, reading, asking questions, studying liturgies, listening, meditating, and participating in celebration as well as lament, often around the table.

Transcendence has taken place as bread has been broken collectively. As Rachel Held Evans shared through her life that "Christianity isn't meant to simply be believed; it's meant to be lived, shared, and enacted in the presence of other people."

This common phrase, "Let's go ahead and put dinner on the table, dad will be home shortly" was spoken daily around 5pm throughout my childhood. This regular gathering through my developmental childhood years allowed me to begin to understand the complexities of the table. Dad and mom, you made this time a priority for our family. Jodi and Joy, you two were the faces I looked at across the table, thank you!

Communication about the table originates with my extended family, each of you have shown up at the table, embody curious conversation, and care for one another. Uncle Len, Aunt Mary Ann, Uncle Jim, Aunt Molly, Scott, Garilyn, Maddie, Lily, Vivian,

Acknowledgments

Emily, Rose, Jen, Anthony, Zion, Grace, Eric, Katie, Brynn, Davis, Paul, Vanessa, Andrew, Kristin, Gabe, Stephen, Tricia, Brennan, Leah, Carson, Owen, Ken, Andrew, and Anya, thank you!

Supportive, wise, patient companions near and far, have been selfless in their belief of this endeavor and it has not gone unnoticed. Joy Hurlow, Jackie White, Tamara and Dr. Chris Bounds, Lauren and Mark Shepherd, Laura and Will Sallee, Haley and Brandon Weaver, Michelle Allen, Ibach family, Kristin and Tyler Green, Bethany Showalter, Katy Longnecker, Trisha Prickett, Kaylyn Moran, Jeannie Banter, Heather Dongell, Jessica Avery, Esther Jadhav, Sarah Baldwin, Brooke Lincoln, Brad Walker, Josie Starkey, Cindy and Jerry Pattengale, Ethan and Sarah Linder, Lauren and Aaron Cloud, Carla and Matt Dyment, Jere Wetherspoon, Jessica and Colin Cassidy, Josh Craton, Katie Rousopoulos, Sara and Travis Hightower-Yoder, Lisa Barber, Nolan and Becca Sponseller, Sarah Beth and Jeff Timmer, Richele Groeneweg, Dara and Jason Berkhalter, Sarah and Brian Jobson, Katie East, Miles Welch, Hayley Morgan, Rachel and Nathan Carlberg, Cicely Wiers-Windemuller, Melissa and Chris Smith, Linda Hundt, Beth and Dale Locke, Tamara Hoffman, and Sarah E. Westfall thank you!

Neighbors met in Upland, your homes offer peaceful space at ever-expanding and transitional tables. You and your families embody the essence of hospitality, Kelly and Brad Yordy, JoAnna and Tyler Witzig, Mel and Scott Barrett, Kate and Steve Austin, Ashely and Troy Tiberi, Bekah and Drew Moser, Gwen and Kevin Diller, Sara and Ryan James, Rachael and Chris DeMarse, Amy Barnett, Jeff and Rachel Aupperle, Lori Slater, Kara and Jon Cavanagh, Kate and Kyle Gould, thank you!

The tables we often share are around discussions and decisions, and on the best days with homemade chai . . . we share a desire to educate for whole person development through transformational discipleship. Bev, Lori, Debby, Chip, Skip, Drew, Scott, Steve, Jeff, Jeff, Kyle, Jon, Kathy, Jennifer, Jesse, Peter, Tyler, Joshua, Jessica, Jessie, Natalie, Josiah, Jana, Kenedy, Serena, Jared, Bailey, Kimie, Shelby, Nick, and Ethan, thank you!

Acknowledgments

In these years of writing, you have sat for more hours than can be counted holding space for the nuances of joy and grief to be simultaneously present. You personify empathy which has ushered in therapeutic healing, thank you!

Setting the table for the Eucharist at College Wesleyan Church has been done with liturgical intentionality, Steve DeNeff, Emily Vermilya, Matt Beck, Jordan and Daniel Rife, thank you!

Academically, you inspired and challenged me, Lori Wagner, Len Sweet, Paul Pastor, Cliff Berger, Loren Kerns, Heather Rainey, Roger Nam, Phil Cranes, Lisa Graham McMinn, and Christine Pohl thank you!

With others, there is deep sadness at the loss of relationship and intertwined hopes for a loving communal life that we shared for so many years. This history together has provided gravity to the understanding of how the Divine intended inclusion, mutuality, and communication within relationship. The three of us have shared many meals together that have shaped what I value about community. Holding gratitude for these memories we have, all the while holding grief that it no longer mutually exists.

Incarnational relationships hold nuances, yet appreciation that the table is a place to gather. Hospitality can be profoundly welcoming at the table! Participation is kneaded and communication is invaluable. I echo the words of Ralph Waldo Emerson, "I awoke this morning with devout thanksgiving for my friends, the old and the new."

Cheers to what has been!

Cheers to what is awaiting!

Part One

Introduction, In the Beginning . . .

Our goal therefore is to learn the curriculum of a truly spiritual life
. . . grounded in love, mercy, tenderness, compassion, forgiveness,
hope, trust, simplicity, silence, peace, and joy. To embody union with
God is to discover these beautiful characteristics emerging from
within and slowly transfiguring us to remake us
in the very image and likeness of God.

CARL MCCOLMAN[1]

In the beginning when God created the heavens and the earth, the
earth was a formless void and darkness covered the face of the deep
while a wind from God swept over the face of the waters.

GENESIS 1:1–2

In the beginning was the Word, and the Word was with God,
and the Word was God.

JOHN 1:1

1. Rohr, "Mysticism: Week 2: Julian of Norwich, Part I," para. 1.

ONCE UPON A TIME. These four words illustrate a genesis. In Scripture, the beginning has an expansive setting full of what is yet to inhabit love, creativity, inclusivity, meaning, purpose, and belonging which will then all be interdependent with one another, bearing the image of the Triune God. Interconnected unity. The poetic Genesis story has so many details that send the imagination reeling.

Words of rhythmic detail depicting the way the earth looked in the garden of Eden have had minds generating all sorts of ideas of what it must have been like when it was created. Hundreds of pieces of art have been designed attempting to depict emotion, capture thoughts, and express the intangible, as well as articulate imagination when it comes to attempting to bring the words of this story into a visualized state. One of the pieces of art from 1612 by Jan Brueghel the Elder entitled "The Garden of Eden" is a tantalizing visual experience of a painting with expansive splendor of her imagination of creation. The Genesis story is one of the most beautiful poems ever written about the intertwined relationship of earth and humans. A collection of words intended to promote shalom among all creation.

Throughout the writings of the Old and New Testament, shalom is used hundreds of times to promote peace, wholeness, restoration, devotion, and creation without defect.[2] Luke 1:79 speaks of "the way of peace." This word "peace," *shalom*, embodies the depiction of creation where all things would glorify the Triune God as well as bear the image that seamlessly embraces love and belonging. Creator God, Jesus, and the Holy Spirit create this intersected oneness of three separate beings.

The poetic language form speaks of the beauty of the elements of light, darkness, separation of water, created land, vegetation, living creatures, and a place where humans were given breath for relationship and responsibility to care for the land they would inhabit. All of the necessities were fashioned and provided for each creature and human for what was needed to thrive.

All was good.

2. Harper, *Very Good Gospel*, 11–12.

All were image bearers of the Triune God.

All were invited to participate in exploration and care for the inhabited space.

All were given communication about freedom and order.

All had choice.

God created humankind in the image of the Divine Trinity and blessed them. This means each were created out of the love of the Divine. Then after making humankind, man and woman, God announced that they were good. Relationships were good and so was the work that was intended to till and care for the land. People were "Made in God's image to live in loving communion with our Maker, we are appointed earthkeepers and caretakers to tend the earth, enjoy it, and love our neighbors. God uses our skills for the unfolding and well-being of his world so that creation and all who live in it may flourish."[3]

The word "good" in the Hebrew, *tov*, represents the interplay between entities as well as the entity itself. There is an interconnected nature present among the earth, individually and collectively good, connected to bear witness to the Triune God and connected to each other.[4]

Yet, when given a choice to stay faithfully connected to the communication that came from the Divine to maintain the boundary, Adam and Eve choose to disrupt the created shalom. This resulted with what is referred to as the fall in subtitles all throughout written versions of the book of Genesis.

In the garden of Eden, after being deceived, which led to going against the communicated instructions given by God to abstain from eating from the fruit of the tree of knowledge of good and evil, Adam and Eve ate the fruit. Once this took place there was a realization of what they had done which led to fear and hiding. Humankind experienced disconnection and dissonance for the first time from one another, from the Triune God, and from oneself. Shalom had been broken.

3. Christian Reformed Church, "7–12 Creation," 10.

4. Harper, *Very Good Gospel*, 30–31.

In the midst of the disrupted peace, God then asked Adam and Eve the question, "Where are you?" The Divine love of God walked towards Adam and Eve when there was disconnection. God initiated restorative connection with humankind.

The space that had been created for people to belong and be loved in relationship was disrupted by choices. Yet, the God who spoke the world into existence initiated exceptional care for humankind through transcendence and came looking for Adam and Eve.

Unification was the intention for humanity from the beginning with the Divine Trinity. Humankind had unbroken connection at the conception of time. Invitation was offered to share a communal space. The opportunity to participate in the bearing of fruit was among the first spoken words of the Divine communicated to humankind. These elements would be the recipe for transfigurational experiences to transcend earth and have union made up of goodness with the Trinity.

In this place of *shalom* in the garden of Eden poem, food was bountiful and one of the first commandments given for enjoyment. There was one limitation in Genesis 2:17 to distance oneself from eating of the prohibited fruit that was a part of the tree of knowledge of good and evil. This said fruit had the power to break connection between God and humankind. Eating was encouraged, yet there were perimeters. After the fruit was consumed by Adam and Eve *shalom* was broken.

The fragmented relationship with humanity and the triune God would seek to be restored throughout the Old Testament when the people of God would render penance for their disobedience by building an altar to offer an animal sacrifice. The altar became a gathering place for restoring relationship with the Divine Creator God. The altar, a table, would be a place set aside to restore relationship.

In the Old Testament, stories are present that recount the gathering of people around the promise of having provision by coming together to eat. Passover, Feast of the Shelters, New Moon feasts, and Jubilee feasts were among a few of the celebrations that were offerings of provision from the Divine God. Manna and quail were seen as rationed daily offerings from heaven for the Israelites in the desert. Ruth, a widow, was invited to a meal by Boaz where she ate until she was satisfied. Elijah received a loaf of bread from a widow with almost empty jars of flour and oil in the midst of a drought. Daniel ate vegetables as a way to connect with God to gain counsel for the days ahead. Food was an essential form of repentance, celebration, and connection.

The stories around elements of the table extend all throughout the New Testament including Jesus' first miracle of turning water to wine at a wedding. The disciples enjoyed breakfast on the beach with Jesus after a long morning of fishing. Thousands of people were fed from the lunch box of a child. Meals were eaten in homes with Jesus alongside tax collectors. Examples of ingredients were common metaphors in Scripture from sowing seeds to the effects of salt and yeast to multiplying fish and loaves.

When it came time for the relationship of humankind with God to be restored, it was done on an altar. When Jesus died on the cross, this was the way to restore the covenant with God, the Lamb of God was crucified in order to offer forgiveness for the sins of all humanity. The altar sacrifice was no longer used as it was in the Old Testament for blood, it was now around a table that people would meet Jesus.

In the New Testament's account of the resurrection, the followers of Jesus went looking for Jesus yet found an empty tomb. The disciples started walking home when Jesus joined them on their walk, but they did not know it was Jesus, and so they kept walking together. Upon their arrival at home, the invitation was extended to Jesus in Luke 24 as this group of people were going to sit down to break bread together. When Jesus took the bread, blessed it, and then broke it, then the eyes of the disciples recognized Jesus.

Jesus revealed himself through transcending the ordinary, revealing his resurrected self by breaking bread at a table.

The early church of Acts, the *ecclesia*, was known for eating and sharing their belongings with one another. The essence of the early church all throughout the book of Acts included breaking bread together. Whether it was sharing the Eucharist or hosting a meal together within their homes, the gathering around breaking bread has been an offering throughout time of connection, reconnection, and remembering since the church began.

What had been the altar of blood sacrifice all throughout the Old Testament became the table of communion for the early church in the New Testament. This is a place of remembrance, forgiveness, and celebration. May this be a place, as Wendell Berry says, to "practice resurrection."[5]

After the resurrection, Jesus sat down and broke bread with his followers. Jesus embodied this practice of sharing a meal time and time again as a way to build into relationship. This practice of gathering together is not a new idea. The table is not a new idea. It has been a place for meaningful connection. It is a part of the story told about what is to come for all of eternity. One of the final promises of the Scriptural narrative in Revelation is a banquet, a feast for celebration. The table mattered at the beginning of time. The table has mattered all throughout history. The table still matters. The table is promised to always matter.

> Come on home, home to me
> And I will hold you in my arms
> And joyful be
> There will always, always be
> A place for you at my table
> Return to me.[6]

---

5. Berry, *Mad Farmer Poems*, 19.

6. Garrels, "At the Table."

Part Two

Longing for Transcendence

My body is what connects me to all of these other people.
Wearing my skin is not a solitary practice but one that brings me
into communion with all these other embodied souls.

BARBARA BROWN TAYLOR[1]

My soul thirsts for God, for the living God.
When shall I come and behold the face of God.

PSALM 42:2

The grace of the Lord Jesus Christ, the love of God,
and the communion of the Holy Spirit be with you all.

2 CORINTHIANS 13:13

TRANSCENDENCE MEANS GOING BEYOND ordinary limits; sur-
passing; exceeding.[2] What thoughts are present when the word
transcendence is heard? What are the feelings that are present

1. Taylor, *An Altar in the World: A Geography of Faith*, 62.

2. "Transcendent," Dictionary.com, accessed February 9, 2020, https://
www.dictionary.com/browse/transcendent.

in your body at the idea of something or someone exceeding the confines of everyday life? What area of life would you welcome transcendence at this time? What do you imagine is necessary for transcendence to take place?

Throughout all the years of humanity's existence there has been a mystery in the soul that longs for meaning, for something to connect with beyond the five senses. People have been looking for the sensation of euphoria through relationships, substances, purchases, and adventures since the poetic beginning of Genesis. A longing for encounters with the Divine Other are a part of humanity's long for the eternal connection to the Triune God.

People talk about experiences that are out of body in a way that alludes to that with which is transcendent. These are moments when it seems that the sacredness of a moment transports beyond the ordinary everyday experiences. Sometimes though, being present for these moments can take place through showing up in the commonality of everyday elements that all of a sudden offer encounters with that which is miraculous. The early church modeled the sharing of meals as a way of life gathering on a regular basis without being pretentious, rather, welcoming.[3]

All are welcome! This is a phrase that people might see on church signs, clothing, or doormats outside of homes. The intention behind these words hold great impact on someone if they are true. To be welcomed somewhere means that there is a place for you to enter as yourself.

Childhood Church on West Cook Road

The church building was a consistent setting for a number of stories that make up my childhood. Participation at these church events were a part of our household routine, a sacred ritual. However, as with anything that is done on a consistent basis, the shimmer, mystery, and wonder were not always present, but I did desire to be faithful in gathering with other Jesus followers that kept my almost

---

3. Pointer Adams, *Wabi-Sabi Welcome*, 34.

perfect attendance all throughout my childhood into my teenage years. Any chance to be at church as well as welcome others to come to church was of utmost importance. The Hurlow family of five were willingly present at church on a regular basis.

One summer, I had the job of cleaning the church building. This was among a myriad of jobs on my high school resume. On this particular day while winding the cord of the vacuum after walking through the rows of pews to make sure there were no crumbs from communion remaining or gum wrappers left behind on the mauve carpet, I walked toward the back of the sanctuary towards the atrium. As I went to turn off the sanctuary lights with one hand and then reach to open the wooden door, my eyes caught the beams of sunlight that were shining through the east side of the stained glassed windows illuminating the pews, altar, and communion table. Each wooden piece was glistening as if a fresh coat of satin stain had just been applied.

I stopped in my freshly vacuumed tracks on the carpet. Something about the transcending light took me by surprise as I had spent a few hours meticulously suctioning up dirt from the carpet in this expansive space and never noticed the sunlight. In that moment of such light, I felt a beckoning that there was more happening than just a weekly vacuuming.

I coiled the vacuum cord into its place in the janitorial closet, recorded the end of my shift on my time card, and returned quietly to the sanctuary to sit in a sunlit pew at the front of the church. The light from the outside had invaded the space that just moments prior had been filled with the ordinary task of vacuuming between wooden benches.

Church pews were a source of measurement throughout my childhood. I remember when my feet went from swinging in the air as I sat as a child to being firmly planted on the ground. These pews and I were well-acquainted; do the math of fifty-two weeks multiplied by seventeen years of my life and voilà, you have at least the number of times I had come to sit on these wooden benches week after week. It was a familiar place to sit, yet I valued its sacred nature in the church. This is where you sat to meet God.

Week to week, about halfway back on the right side facing the stage, was the place where you could spot the Hurlow family. This pew, probably around row "P" if the sanctuary would have been lettered like a stadium, was where the season-ticket holders for the members of the Hurlow family sat. Behind us sat the Long family; we all showed up weekly to those seats for the 10:30 AM service. Except for my mom, that is. She sang in the choir, so she would come sit with us after the choir sang the musical number for that week, usually after the ushers took the tithes and offerings and right before the pastor started preaching. Or some weeks there would be a special number by a church member, one of my personal favorites was Janet's rendition of "His Eye Is on the Sparrow" which was a regular in the lineup.

There were plenty of seats in this large sanctuary, full of wooden pews.

In addition to all of the rows of seating, there were two kneeling altars in the front of the church, easy access from any of the three aisles. Alas, "the altar was always open" at church. There was not a Sunday that went by that that phrase was not recited by someone from the pulpit. You could come, sit, or kneel at any point in the service and be guaranteed that a prayer saint would get down on their knees to pray with you. I am not sure exactly what people prayed, but it always looked comforting to know you had someone next to you. People went up weekly and it looked like a meaningful place to encounter the Eternal Other by participating in prayer.

Another form of participation that took place was through the invitation to partake of monthly communion. On the altar, on the first Sunday of each month, the shiny gold-looking platters were stacked with the communion elements. The wafers lay on a white flowery doily in the center and the small, individual plastic cups of store-bought grape juice were held in cupholders on the outer ring of the platter.

The items that sat on the communion table held communication of celebration, lament, and remembering. These elements were front and center in the church. The placement held intentionality; they were central to being a Jesus follower.

The wood grain on this communion table was stunning. On the other Sundays, there was often a lit candle along with a large Bible laying open to a passage with a promise. At times the local florist brought lilies or poinsettias that were ornamental to the coinciding holiday, bought in memory of a congregant. On the Sundays when a fresh planter was setting on the communion table altar, it was a reminder to the congregation of a recent life who had passed away.

I went to a lot of funerals as a child; my parents believed that showing up to support people who are grieving was very important and so those experiences would come with questions about the meaning of life. Jeff Chu, reporter and editor, writes, "Soil holds both hope and grief. It's where we grow and where we bury. It carries the promise and possibility of life and the memory and legacy of death."[4]

Grief and hope sat side by side on the altar, a table with assigned seats, and both were welcomed. It was the death and resurrection of Jesus that was represented. Both invited remembrance and redemption through this rhythm around this sacred ritual.

On this particular summer day, something was transcending the orderliness.

There was a brief moment of sitting in the rays of sunlight when I wanted to take off my shoes in solidarity with Moses. As I sat down in the front pew with the stained glass window on my right there was only a sunbeam between me, the communion table, and the altar.

The veil was thin between heaven and earth that afternoon. The path was lit, marked with accessibility to move towards what was truly meaningful as a Jesus follower; to encounter the communion table as a place that could offer convergence, not just the Sundays when the gold platters of wafer and juice were present. It was as if on this particular day the herald of angels were singing

---

4. Chu, "Photo of Soil in Planter."

with a peaceful chorus for earth, you belong here! Come to the table and while you are at it, have others join too!

The Yearning for Meaning and Belonging

To have a place to go with questions is of great significance because these inquires come with desires to transcend a current situation in order to encounter another one. For there to be space for communication about that which is unknown is stabilizing for relationship. An age-old question, "what is the meaning of life," is as ever-present as the rising and setting of the sun among humanity. Meaning often originates when people feel a sense of belonging. People spend significant time investing in the places, people, and activities where they find meaning and a sense of belonging. People invite people into what is important to them, they show up ready to participate, and spend hours communicating about its importance. Why then is there a decline in society for people to feel as if they have belonging and are connected?

People derive shades of identity and meaning from the many facets of life, the places in which there is an investment of time and energy. Relationships form with the resonance of mutual interest and values and also provide common identifiers. Groups, educational pursuits, clubs, school districts, and leagues are where people come together with shared interest to build belonging, which offers a sense of connection.

Some people find belonging in positions of prominence. Participation in prestigious board meetings around conference tables is not the sole place for wisdom to be found; the daily practice of gathering at the kitchen table can offer wisdom that transcends. This space can then create a setting that touches the earth for meaningful connection in relationships to be nourished with a sense of value and belonging.

There is an opportunity to have a relaxed sense of self when someone knows that they are welcome to belong, by just showing up as themselves. Belonging is integral to our understanding of what we believe and it has been since the beginning.[5] Behavior is externalizing what we understand about our belonging and belief.

The Old Testament

In the Old Testament, YHWH is the one who hosted and provided common meals for all of creation, both animals and humans.[6] The altar was a space for offering a sacrifice as a means of repentance and a place to remember the covenant God made with all of humanity. An altar was a place where people made vows of commitment in front of God, each other, and their community. This was a way to enact participation in the faithfulness of God. *Hesed* is the Hebrew word that represents the covenant of loving-kindness, mercy, and loyalty from Yahweh God to humanity.[7]

The covenant of faithfulness is an ongoing promise for humanity. Creation bears the likeness of the trinity of God, Jesus, and the Holy Spirit; understanding this foundational truth gives insight into the faithfulness of God.[8] In order to understand the table it is important to contextualize the formation of communion throughout the Scripture narrative.

After an altar experience took place, the table was set as a means to participate in *hesed*.[9] The altar in the Old Testament depicts blood sacrifices, followed by a meal together. Exodus 24:11 shares that after Moses encountered God through the blood covenant, "they beheld God, and they ate and drank." Following the meal, a cleansing and forgiveness took place. "The blood of the covenant establishes our relationship with God so that we may eat in his presence as we affirm our allegiance to the covenant,

5. Heuertz, *Enneagram of Belonging*, 31.

6. MacDonald, *What Did the Ancient Israelites Eat?*, xv.

7. Strong, *New Strong's Expanded Exhaustive Concordance of the Bible*, 93.

8. Hicks, *Come to the Table*, 14–15.

9. Hicks, *Come to the Table*, 28–31.

participate in the forgiveness of that altar, and experience the presence of God at the table."[10]

To engage in table celebrations after an altar experience was a joyful expression of the covenantal love that was a symbol of renewal of union with God and others. There are multiple stories of this renewal in the Old Testament: entering into the Promised Land in Joshua 8, sacrificing offerings at the completion of the temple in 2 Chronicles 7:10, and rebuilding the temple after there had been captivity in Babylon in Ezra 6. The feasts of the Old Testament represent the joining around a table to acknowledge renewal that was taking place with God.[11]

The table is a place for joy and communion in the presence of God. At the table, "God is a participant because he is a party to the covenant . . . God shares his holy presence with his people and renews his own commitment to his people."[12] God was present at the meals shared with Israel and in sending Jesus Christ to earth, God manifests presence in order to eat with the people in the New Testament.

The New Testament

God communicated that the identity formed around the table with creation was a response to the covenant: all receive an invitation to come and receive the provisions, to come, and break bread together. Dr. Constance Cherry, a professor in the area of church worship, has further expounded in her writing that "In the first sixteen centuries of Christianity (both East and West), communing at the Table of the Lord was a normative response to the word. Spending time at the table was a symbolic way to recreate the message of Christ through our senses: dramatic action, and symbolic gesture."[13] There are meals permeating through the

10. Hicks, *Come to the Table*, 33.

11. Hicks, *Come to the Table*, 33–37.

12. Hicks, *Come to the Table*, 36.

13. Cherry, *Worship Architect*, 86–87.

New Testament, from feeding of thousands to the passing of the Eucharist. The shared table, as Nathan MacDonald, a Scottish Biblical scholar, would say, "has decisive significance in the early Christ-movement. Meals are seen as loci of identity formation and transformation."[14]

The meals continued as Jesus broke bread with individuals and large groups of people throughout his lifetime on earth. During the Last Supper, Jesus modeled communion with his disciples including Judas, who would betray him within hours of that shared meal.[15] Communion at the Last Supper marked the beginning of the Eucharist for the *ecclesia*, the early church of the New Testament. They implemented communion as a sacrament for future generations. Both people who loved Jesus and would later betray Jesus came together around the table to experience the breaking of the bread.

In the account of the Last Supper (Matthew 26:17–30), Jesus models that true communion is not just to drink of the wine and eat the bread, it is experienced by sharing meals together. The table was not just about communion with God. Rather, sitting at a table is a commitment to serve those sharing the table with you. It is to participate with the other people present. The moments shared together are mutual commitment and care. The table involves interaction between God and people as well as among the people present at the table.[16]

Communal restoration is needed at the table. The intention around the table was to experience belonging and meaningful connection. The genesis of the table was to participate in union with God and simulatenously share with other people to bring covenant relationship into daily life.

The table is a place where people can come as invited guests to participate with God in the very nourishment of a mutual covenantal relationship. It is a place to model Trinitarian values by

---

14. MacDonald, *What Did the Ancient Israelites Eat?*, xvii.

15. MacDonald, *What Did the Ancient Israelites Eat?*, 67.

16. MacDonald, *What Did the Ancient Israelites Eat?*, 80–81.

imitating them in daily life.[17] This communal act bears the image of the Triune God manifested in human interaction interdependent of one another.

The Eucharist is an opportunity to offer a response of gratitude in the conventional commitment. While the experience is a divine act, it is nevertheless also a human need. It is a human affirmation of covenantal commitment and thanksgiving. When we eat and drink, we commit ourselves to the values of the Gospel, which the meal embodies. We offer thanks for divine grace. Through the participation, we commit ourselves to God and to each other. When we sit at table with Jesus who humbled himself to give his life for others, we commit ourselves to the humble service of others, even to the point of giving our lives (and belongings) for each other. Eating and drinking without commitment is to eat and drink judgment, but to eat and drink with commitment is to visibly take up your cross at the table and follow Jesus.[18]

In following the way of Jesus, by breaking bread at the table, there is recognition that the host is present as the living God. "The present table is a foretaste of the eschatological table in the new heaven and new earth where God will fully dwell with his people as their God. There the goal of God is fully accomplished and God sits at table with his people as he always intended."[19] The Spirit of the Living God will bring reformation and renewal to the conflict that has created disunity around the table. When unity takes place, the restoration as image bearers of the Triune God enhances the identity of Jesus' followers.

It is imperative to understand what is keeping people from coming to the table. There is fear of exposure in the vulnerability of yearning for meaning and belonging, lack of faith identification, as well as the decline in a communal identity around a table; these are all contributing factors for why people do not come to the table. Yet, at the same time, there is a desire that people have to be seen, known, and loved, which offers a place for belonging.

17. MacDonald, *What Did the Ancient Israelites Eat?*, 112.

18. MacDonald, *What Did the Ancient Israelites Eat?*, 148.

19. MacDonald, *What Did the Ancient Israelites Eat?*, 149.

This is a desire for a transfigurational experience around the table with other people while breaking bread that continues to tell the Genesis story of when God said it was good in the garden for people to be together; this has been a part of the human story since time began.

Jesus Followers

Jesus followers believe there is belonging and connection because it is the essence of the larger narrative of Scripture. In Genesis 1:27, the poetic story shares the creation of human beings is done so in God's image; people derive identity as human beings as image bearers of the Triune God.

From the beginning, this relationship with God has defined a people who all identify as "holy."[20] The Jewish tradition, our foundational heritage, has passed on this identity through story, Scripture, song, and table. As Anita Diamant, an author of a number of books on Jewish history and tradition, states, "Home is where the heart is, where tastes are shaped, where the eye first focuses, where identity is forged. In the Jewish tradition, home is a mikdash ma'at, little sanctuary. The holy of holies."[21]

Out of this tradition, the sacrifice and resurrection of Jesus the Messiah, a Christian church was born, one that identified itself in the worship of the Triune God. The identity of this new church is in believing in the Truth of a present and powerful Jesus who could transfigure lives, offer forgiveness and hope. There is hope for those who will embody the incarnation in order to offer healing, joy, and peace to one another.

Early church followers of Jesus were called the gathering of those anointed by the Holy Spirit, the *ecclesia*. A community infused by the Holy Spirit broke bread while learning together to create a strong identity of inclusion and belonging. The power and

20. 1 Peter 1:15–17.
21. Diamant and Kushner, *How to Raise a Jewish Child*, 17.

redemptive hope of Jesus offered connection and meaning that mirrored the Trinitarian love of the *Imago Dei*.

The table here on earth is a place for gathering, remembering, eating, feasting, discussing, as well as worshiping. Gordon Smith offers insight into the first meals of Scripture by saying, "the meal is a central motif in the Bible."[22] Ecclesiastes 10:19 shares about food by stating, "Feasts are made for laughter; wine gladdens life." Psalm 34:8 uses our sense of taste to share about the goodness of God by saying, "O taste and see that the Lord is good; happy are those who take refuge in him." God is continually offering unending love even through daily provisions.

Jesus' lifestyle consistently experienced enjoyment with people who opened up their homes for meals all the while offering hospitality to him as he was on his journey. Jesus' practices of eating with other people along with praying about daily nourishment offers a portrait of how he viewed integration of these practices.[23] "Give us each day our daily bread," Luke 11:3.[24] Jesus ate with the purpose of sharing.[25] The opportunity to learn from the Biblical narrative can have profound impact on the way that the western culture in the 21st century lives life. The sharing of stories with intentionality, creativity, and integration retell the story of the redemptive Gospel.

The embodiment of this connected identity, as Jesus followers, has been the infrastructure for a solidarity in gathering around the table by sharing the Eucharist and breaking bread together. The space then becomes a sacred place for learning collectively.[26]

The essentials of the table included sharing bread and wine in the name of Jesus. This practice of sharing these elements constitute a committed relationship with the trinity. In the breaking of bread and sharing of wine, an identity as a Jesus follower formed, and a deep and relational commitment was continually renewed

22. Smith, *Holy Meal*, 11.

23. LaVerdiere, *Dining in the Kingdom of God*, 9.

24. LaVerdiere, *Dining in the Kingdom of God*, viii.

25. Stookey, *Eucharist*, 20–21.

26. Böckmann, *Around the Monastic Table*, 183.

through the rhythmic practice. As the *ecclesia* met together on a regular basis to break bread, as described in Acts 2:46 and 5:42, the early church grew. Although there were disagreements among people, there was a significant regard for oneness, which encouraged people to be together as one body of believers.[27]

The Eucharist is central to experiencing the transcendence of the Divine through remembering, thanksgiving, and celebration. As Henri Nouwen wrote, "The Lord is the center of all things and yet in such a quiet, unobtrusive, elusive way. He lives with us, even physically, but not in the same physical way that other elements are present to us. The transcendent physical presence is what characterizes the Eucharist."[28] The bond is invisible, but if it takes place with other humans, it also allows for transcendence among incarnational communities.

However, the Church has been slowly losing its identity. This relationship of lost identity has had a strong connection to the failure of the church to tend and till relationships, as well as to pass the faith on to children and others. There has been a loss of emphasis on the table as a place of significance in the home, church, and community. To break bread together is to reclaim the spoken story of Jesus' transfigurational power. The spoken word was what "broke the silence" of the world when God initiated the creation of the earth. There was a power present in the spoken word that has been a part of the oral tradition of learning for years. "The psychological effect of the living voice is the creation of a sense of presence and power."[29] The spoken word has been a part of the faith narrative tradition since the beginning. It is important to recognize that the table is a gathering place where people can join together to audibly speak and share the Truth-filled messages of the historical-biblical narrative.[30]

Changing cultural patterns with more activities, events, and opportunities along with the distance people travel for work, have challenged humanity's ability to share space at the table. The choices

27. Ladd, *Young Church*, 64–65.

28. Nouwen, *Eternal Seasons*, 187.

29. Lischer, *Theology of Preaching*, 50.

30. Lischer, *Theology of Preaching*, 50–53.

humanity has made affect the church by hindering regular times of sharing space around the table. This lack of time spent together has impacted the sharing of the Larger story of faith around the table.

It is important to acknowledge the historical Scriptural importance and the identity formation of sharing bread and wine, along with the neighborhood importance of sharing the table with others. This then can communicate that there is a present day opportunity for a transfigurational experience with the Triune God that takes place by breaking bread together wherever the table is located.

The *ecclesia* of the first century was made of people of the New Testament era who were called out of their way of living to follow a new way of the redemptive message of Jesus Christ. In the time of gathering, bread was broken to share the story of the gospel. In the book of Matthew, the reference to breaking of bread and drinking from the cup was symbolic to communion, as it was a continual metaphor throughout Scripture.[31] In Acts, the *ecclesia* built their houses with enough space for tables for gathering together for meals on a regular basis.[32] When people gathered to break bread they were nourishing their bodies physically, and simultaneously embodying the story of Jesus' body broken to set people free through his resurrection. Breaking bread together is a way to share the story of Jesus' death and resurrection through participation with others by embodying and retelling the redemption story of the gospel.

As the story of Scripture concludes, the final invitation in the book of Revelation is for people to come and drink the water of life.[33] There is continually an invitation to come, partake, and receive. Throughout Scripture, the Triune God set the table for us to partake, but people must make the choice to come to the table.

A transfigurational experience around the meal table on a daily basis, with a strong lyrical tempo of transformation, can shape people into the image of the Triune God. In order for this

31. Matthew 26:26.

32. Acts 2:47, 20:11.

33. Revelation 22:17.

to happen, people have the opportunity to experience genuine relationship with the Triune God through invitation, participation, and communication around the table with others by breaking bread together on a consistent basis.

As a multiple-time-a-week churchgoing kid, engaging in the fifteen minutes a month devoted to the Eucharist was ceremonial to repent of my sins in order to be in right relationship with God. Breaking bread together and drinking grape juice, disguised for wine, was a once-a-month sacramental ritual tacked onto the end of the Sunday morning service. This happened twelve times a year, yet I remember longing for this to happen more consistently as a rhythm for sharing the sacrament as a way to engage relationship.

Daniel Rife, codirector of worship arts at College Wesleyan Church, shares wisdom on the sacramental worship of the Eucharist, "The sacrament of the Eucharist is the experience of Christ being present around the table with others. It is Emmanuel, God with you, in a tangible way. He is here and he is aware of you. To participate in the Eucharist is to recognize there are implications upon building an identity in reflection of God's power."[34]

Storytelling Around the Table

When something takes place on a regular basis, there is an opportunity to develop a consistent rhythm that can build a robust story. That is why the opportunity to utilize the table daily, integrating the practice of breaking bread and drinking wine as a way of coming together, can go beyond just the repentance needed to restore relationship. It can be a way for reflection to offer thanksgiving, and celebrate God's relationship to us as well as our relationship with others.

In the book, *From Tablet to Table: Where Community is Found and Identity is Formed*, Leonard Sweet offers an overarching perspective of the effects on identity from time shared around a table. "If we were to make the table the most sacred object of furniture in

---

34. Daniel Rife, interviewed by author, Marion, Indiana, on March 3, 2017.

every home, in every church, in every community, our faith would quickly regain its power, and our world would quickly become a better place. The table is the place where identity is born—the place where the story of our lives is retold, re-minded, and relived."[35] People are bountiful fields of stories waiting for harvest.

Stories are the blood that keeps the oxygen flowing from generation to generation. The oral culture of sharing the story of the Scripture has been present since the beginning of time. Seeing is believing on an entirely different level when it comes to archeology. Often in an archeological dig, the foundation is what is found. Many times the walls or exterior elements have been destroyed, but places can be identified by their foundation.

The table is a foundational location for sharing stories. Sweet articulates, "At the table, where food and stories are passed from one person to another and one generation to another, is where each of us learns who we are, where we come from, what we can be, to whom we belong, and to what we were called."[36]

The identity formation that takes place through sharing space and stories around the table is experiencing crisis in a time of history when one in five meals per week is eaten in the car.[37] The time that people spend eating meals in front of a screen or without anyone else around during mealtime is on the rise in many cultures. There is concern regarding this form of meal-eating behavior because it does not promote the intentions of Jesus' life on earth as it pertained to breaking bread.[38] The meal was intended to savor, enjoy, and promote communion with other people.

Jesus' intentions orient communally, which promote identity formation around the story of the Triune God. The table is intended to be shared collectively. For Jesus followers, this embodies the representation as image bearers of the Trinitarian relationship around a meal. Your table becomes the preeminent art of your

---

35. Sweet, *From Tablet to Table*, 2–3.

36. Sweet, *From Tablet to Table*, 8.

37. Sweet, *From Tablet to Table*, 9.

38. Sweet, *From Tablet to Table*, 11–13.

life. You become a disciple to the Master Artist through your time spent together at Jesus' table.[39]

The stories that people embody are as vast as the horizon and as expansive as the galaxies. Throughout church history, stories continue to be experienced around the table, where people are breaking bread together. Sweet says, "When you tell a story, you are transferring your experiences directly to the brains of those listening; they feel what you feel, think what you think, smell what you smell. You are teleporting your story to their brain."[40] The individual stories of Jesus followers are pointing to the larger narrative of the Triune God.

To engage in the larger story of the Triune God, people must acknowledge the need for identity formation and its rootedness around sharing stories at the table. The intentional act of breaking bread is for people to experience the embodiment of what Jesus gave to his disciples, "storied identity—meaning that he framed their identity in the stories he told as he walked about, healed, and taught in ancient Palestine."[41] This enhancement of understanding of identity around the table is a way to model the life of a Jesus follower through being a host, a guest, as well as someone who welcomes strangers, friends, and enemies.

A few years ago while walking the Camino Primitivo in Spain, I noticed there was a regularity to the days of walking alone or among fellow travelers on the trail day in and day out. The Camino, translated "path," had a number of differing routes that people from all over the world would walk towards in order to reach the city of Santiago de Compostela. Each day along the path would be albergues, also known as pilgrim houses, where guests were welcomed in whatever state we found ourselves. Someone would greet us with a resounding hola! Instantaneously there were gracious instructions as we were disrobing our hiking packs, trekking poles, and taking off our shoes, which had been the cocoon for our feet for the entirety of the day. We were welcomed to come sit down

39. Sweet, *From Tablet to Table*, 18.
40. Sweet, *From Tablet to Table*, 33.
41. Sweet, *From Tablet to Table*, 49.

and within moments, crusty bread with jamón and cheese on it were in front of us with a glass of wine. To say, "oh, gracias!" was met with a simple, "de nada." This would be said to imply this is no big deal, and "it is nothing." The hosts were generously hospitable with spoken words and loving actions.

The reception that was offered at the end of each day was one of celebration. The feeling of hospitality was offered and the concept of mi casa es su casa was experienced. We ended our days of hiking with people who welcomed us to come and rest in the care of kind hosts.

To love another is to experience the core identity of the Triune God. As Kierkegaard so eloquently shares, "He who cannot reveal himself cannot love, and he who cannot love is the most unhappy man of all."[42] To engage in love for another around the shared space at the table where conversations are not limited and silence is welcomed when needed, means that there can be a healing balm for people to process their emotion, thoughts, and experiences.

As the evolution of a Jesus follower's identity unfolds around the table, the sincerity of hospitality is of utmost importance. Sweet summarizes this art in a profoundly beautiful way by sharing, "I used to think hospitality was a lost art. Now I am convinced it is a lost heart."[43] To offer from a person's heart is an outpouring of one's core, it is courageous.[44] The identity formation of the heart happens around a table.

There is a need for Jesus followers to embody the orthopraxy around the table. Engaging in storytelling is formational to building identity around the table, all the while there must be practicalities to this in one's life on a consistent basis. Interacting with other people through conversation is communication that can offer understanding of individual experiences. The opportunity to take turns listening can help people know one another in ways that can lead to truth-telling.

42. Flynn, *Existentialism: A Very Short Introduction*, 32.

43. Flynn, *Existentialism: A Very Short Introduction*, 138.

44. Brown, *I Thought It Was Just Me (But It Isn't): Making the Journey from "What Will People Say" to "I am Enough.")*, xxiii.

My earliest memories of identity, meaning, and belonging are around a table. I remember times spent around the table with people from multiple generations. This was during late fall, with the transitioning of clothed trees to naked ones covering the ravine in our middle-America town. The pumpkins, dry cornhusks, and straw bales awaited their Thanksgiving Day front door debut before the accents of Advent and all its Fraser fir pine-scented décor would take center stage. I hold sacred this memory of gathering together with others around a table because it was telling a story of our family that reenacted the larger story of people coming together. There was always a plate ready for each person who was coming, each person had a place of belonging at the table. There was an invitation for each person to join and partake in the breaking of bread, which concluded in the form of Aunt Jill's cut out cookies.

The table was set with dried apple decorations and hand painted ceramic figurines spaced out along the beautifully ironed white tablecloths. Alongside the distinct memorabilia from childhood art class, the table was embedded with a variety of family members' and friends' narratives. Name tags were set with intention as each had responded to the invitation of the hosts, my gracious aunt and uncle. The tradition of circling up around the large table to share in a blessing, hymn, and prayer was as natural as taking one's place in a team huddle before the big game. Reaching for the hand of the one next to you, held with care, symbolized a time of gathering relationships together to offer reflective thankfulness. Breaking bread together, as well as listening to each other's stories, can knit their experiences of sorrows and celebrations together from the previous year as well as the Triune God's provisions. People graciously offered stories of gratitude and redemption. This gathering reflected the imagery of the Trinitarian relationship of mutual love and belonging that humanity was created to experience.

A gathering of many people sharing stories represents the larger narrative of Scripture, exchanging experiences around belonging and the Truth. As Rachel Held Evans has said, "It's easier to remember things together than alone."[45] Stories are shared as each takes time to remember how they have come to this space together, along with words of thanksgiving spoken with gratitude.

The November holiday table is set yearly, inviting each person to participate in remembering, thanks-giving, and celebrating together, able to worship the Triune God through relationship.

I remember the meals when we have come around the Thanksgiving table and shared tearful conversations about losses throughout the past year. I remember when life choices led to painful consequences that were less than ideal.

One year my cousin shared his story of falling in love and proceeded to pass around the dazzling diamond ring that would be a part of an upcoming engagement proposal. I was awestruck as a young girl by this profound love and celebrated the joyful event that would take place. I can vividly remember the pregnancy announcements of new family members, travel opportunities, along with jobs offered that further promoted skills. Stories rooted in sheer joy and celebration.

There have also been times over tears as people have shared about the waiting that they are experiencing in their lives. For a child. For adventure. For a different job. For wisdom. For a life partner. For patient endurance. For redemption. Sharing stories of desire, along with the not yet, made it clear this space was a welcoming place for wherever people are in their story.

Yet, this is just one day of the year. I long for this experience to be more than just one celebration a year. There is a longing for meaningful belonging that is telling the relational story of the Triune God on a daily basis. What took place around the Thanksgiving table once a year, along with the first Sunday of the month's Eucharistic ritual, were formational and sacred to my understanding of origin story of how the *ecclesia* came together.

Jesus brings humanity into communion with the Triune God and each other through sharing in the Eucharist.[46] Experiencing

45. Evans, *Searching for Sunday: Loving, Leaving, and Finding the Church*, 128.

46. Vander Zee, *Christ, Baptism, and the Lord's Supper: Recovering the*

the breaking of bread around a table on a regular basis offers a sacred rhythm to individual lives as they come together as image bearers of the Triune God. To engage in soulful nourishment as well as physical nourishment among others is a transfigurational opportunity. The soulful cultivation can take place when people respond to the invitation.

Proximity to Another

Practical elements are present when it comes to sharing stories and activities with people around us. A table in one's front yard could provide a space for people to gather spontaneously in the neighborhood. In Kristin Schell's thoughtful writing she says, "The Turquoise Table offers simplicity. It is more than a table; it's a symbol of reaching out and making room without all the fuss and frenzy."[47] It is a place to sit down with one another and participate in day-to-day life with those who live in proximity. So often people live in neighborhoods for years and never get to know the stories of the people they cross paths with on a daily basis.

Francis Schaeffer, theologian and founder of L'Abri Community shares, "Don't start with a big program . . . Start personally and start in your home. I dare you. I dare you in the name of Jesus Christ. Begin by opening your home for community. All you have to do is open your home and begin."[48] Over ninety times in Scripture there is instruction on welcoming and caring for a stranger.[49] As a Jesus follower, there is an invitation in James 1:27 to offer care for the orphan and the widow. As people who yearn to belong, know, and be known by neighbors we also have a sacred

---

Sacraments for Evangelical Worship, 199.

47. Schell, *The Turquoise Table: Finding Community and Connection in Your Own Front Yard*, 9.

48. Schell, *The Turquoise Table: Finding Community and Connection in Your Own Front Yard*, 37.

49. Welcoming the Stranger, World Relief, "Scripture and Immigration," accessed September 9, 2017, http://welcomingthestranger.com/wp_welcoming/learn-and-discern/scripture-and-immigration.

responsibility. We must begin with a simple prayer: "Here I am, God. Give me eyes to see."[50]

Where people are in juxtaposition with others there are "rhythms and cadence" to how people live out their routines.[51] A beautiful Irish proverb articulates space by saying, "It is in the shelter of each other that people live." When people have space to express, articulate, and share their stories with others there is a sense of life breathed into interdependent relationships. This is where people know where they end and another person begins, without being co-dependent of one another, they are able to bear meaning together.

Throughout history it is clear that the table has held a meaningful place in Scripture and still is a present day icon. The depiction of the scriptural recognition of the table stands out as a marker of importance. Simultaneously, the formation of one's identity through storytelling around the table as it pertains to sharing the narrative of Scripture is a part of the enactment of taking the communion bread and wine with others gathering together.

The formation around the table is not limited to communion, it can be experienced around the table sharing a meal among neighbors, friends, and family in proximity. It is profoundly loving to offer an invitation to people to know and be known by others living in proximity.

In order to build one's identity as a Jesus follower, there needs to be time and energy spent towards establishing oneself by engaging in the essential practice of breaking bread around the table in order to experience the transcendence in which humanity was created to embody. This offers an opportunity to experience the transfigurational nourishment of the relational Triune God with other people, on a regular basis, in a proximal space.

50. Schell, *The Turquoise Table: Finding Community and Connection in Your Own Front Yard*, 37.

51. Schell, *The Turquoise Table: Finding Community and Connection in Your Own Front Yard*, 93.

Lack of Faith Identification

The longing for meaning and belonging affects the identification that individuals have with faith. "Based on Barna's most recent data, almost four in 10 (38%) Americans are active churchgoers, slightly more (43%) are unchurched, and around one-third (34%) are dechurched. But . . . there are great variations among American cities."[52]

People are not attending church on a regular basis, even though the desire to be a part of a community is present; people are looking for authentic relationships with others. John Eldredge, an author and speaker, shares,

> The church is not a building. Church is not an event that takes place on Sundays. Much to our surprise, that is not how the Bible uses the term. When the Scripture talks about church, it means *community*. The little fellowships of the heart that are outposts of the kingdom. A shared life. They worship together, eat together, pray for one another, and go on quests together. They hang out together, in each other's homes. When Peter is sprung from prison, "he went to the house of Mary the mother of John . . . where many people had gathered and were praying" (Acts 12:12).[53]

Gathering can take place in a variety of places to experience community if the intention of the time is to enact the practices of the love and belonging. Stories can be shared when there is sincerity present.

The table is a structure, a space for sharing faith stories on a regular basis. People experience a form of identity and meaning by the stories they generate. The definition of a Jesus follower comes from the story of the Trinity's relationship to humanity throughout history.[54] William Willimon, a theologian, writes, "People tell stories not simply to give themselves something to do while they

---

52. "Church Attendance Trends around the Country," para. 3.

53. Eldredge, *Waking the Dead*, 192.

54. Sweet, *From Tablet to Table*, 3.

eat, but because stories are important parts of the communion, fellowship, love, joy, and remembrance which make up the mystery of the meal."[55]

To identify with a community of faith offers meaning and a sense of belonging. The following story offers an insightful perspective from a professor who shares from her own vivid experience of growing up in the church and its impact on the way she perceives engaging with the table as a means of bringing people together.

> As a child growing up in a mainline, high church tradition, I was taught a great reverence of the Lord's Table. While I can't say I was never caught running or causing mischief in the sanctuary of that stately church, I'm certain such behavior never made its way near the altar. It was as if there was an invisible fence surrounding the chancel and the table of the Lord and I was the proud owner of the electric shock collar, keeping me at an arm's distance from this holy, sacred space. I remember, on more than one occasion, being dared by the Pastor's kids or my Sunday school buddies to run up and touch the altar cloth; but I was always too intimidated and never acted on the dare. Outside of approaching the table with my parents to receive a blessing from the Pastor while they received communion, the altar was forbidden and uncertain territory.
>
> My sense of reverence for the table was high, to say the least. To that end, I had some level of fear and trepidation upon approaching the altar for my first communion as a teenager. The imaginary, electric shock collar had been removed, but my sense that this space was holy and off-limits still lingered in my heart. I remember anxiously climbing the steps toward the space around the table where I would be offered the bread and the cup. While the room was anything but quiet, I heard nothing but my own breathing and my heavy and uncertain steps toward my destination. This was serious business. And now that I was allowed to come to the table, I was unsure of how it should be engaged . . .

55. Willimon, *Sunday Dinner*, 11.

The truth is, the table of God is many things. It *is* a place to be solemn and to remember the sacrifice of Christ made on our behalf. But it's also a place to give thanks, celebrating the grace and love extended to us by the Father, through the Son, in the power of the Holy Spirit. And it is the place where, together, we are unified, as a body, through God's gifts which are offered freely to us all.[56]

A part of the sacredness of the table is because it is offered freely to all. All are welcome.

Coming to The Lord's table to break bread together can offer an opportunity for people to come with questions, desires, hopes, longings, and individuality to form a faith identity rooted in the narrative of the transfigured Christ. This then allows an extension of the *ecclesia* to form around the table breaking bread together and sharing in the equity modeled by the Triune God in the home.

The Decline in Familial Identity Around a Table

There has been a significant decline in familial and communal identity around the table in recent years. The makeup of a family has expanded from only referring to a dad, mom, and children to including a number of other relational connections in a home. It could be said that today, a modern day family meal consists of those who most often spend time sharing a meal together, yet do not have to sleep in the same house to be considered "family."

Sharing space around a table with people who are not biological family members can create a space of expansion to include other people who we love. I sit at some tables where I am known as Miss Julia, or others identify me as Mimi, while there are others who call me Jules; or I am considered a daughter, friend, sister, niece, coworker, or auntie. Each of these spaces hold a space for belonging to be called by name.

In the Western culture, all too often a sense of security has been limited to a narrow structure that is only made up of immediate family. This arrangement can be detrimental to creating

56. Vermilya, "This Is the Feast," paras. 1–2, 8.

the structure that is needed for people to sense a place of belonging.[57] The pressure that is put upon a relational structure of just birth family does not mirror how Scripture uses familial language around friends as brothers and sisters. The table is wide for relationship as it can offer an array of flavorful personalities coming together to form belonging together.

Sharing a meal with other people can be psychologically reassuring.[58] The television portrays some families who do not eat together, yet others often are sharing family prayers and stories around the table which can appear idyllic. People are craving relational intimacy and connectedness around meals.[59]

Mealtime preparations have changed throughout time as accessibility to food has become easier and appliances have become more efficient at expediting food preparation. Electrical ovens, microwaves, instant pots, drive through restaurants, food delivery, and call-ahead pickup have eliminated the need for people to spend hours preparing food together. There were historical times when food sources were grown, ingredients gathered, and at times cooking it over an open fire. This extensive process would allow for a social connection to be a byproduct of the production of the meal shared together.

All the while, eating three meals a day is a challenge for many based on schedules, social responsibilities, and scattered demands that do not include a shared meal with others. The routine that is often found in Western culture, or lack of one, does not consistently include eating with other people as in previous generations, when specifically Sunday noon was time for people to gather after church for a meal. William Willimon shares this about his experience around the table as a child,

> Sunday meal time was a ritual. Because of this, no one had to tell me what it meant to be a part of this family. I never got formal instruction in orthodox belief of behavior. No one had to explain to me that I belonged or that I

57. Fieldhouse, "Eating Together."
58. Willimon, *Sunday Dinner*, 4.
59. Sweet, *From Tablet to Table*, 11.

was loved. I learned all that at the Sunday dinner table. If someone had asked me, "Who are you people and what do they stand for?" I would have responded quite honestly, "My people are those who gather at grandmother's dinner table." At that table we were initiated, nurtured, and claimed in the family. There we participated in common memory, fellowship, and identity. There we found our place, our name, our story—at the table.[60]

Quite a few people think of an inter-generational group of people sharing a meal for an event like a holiday, celebration, or reunion. However, how often do people think back to where the shared table came from in a historical context? It has been around since the beginning of time. People have been coming together to share meals for generations.[61] Eating together has been a formational place of education since the Genesis poem as it offers a variety of recipes for people to learn how to interact with one another.

Whether it is a picnic table, a church fellowship hall set up with folding tables, a front porch, or a dining room within a house, there is something about sharing a meal that unifies people. When people plant, grow, and harvest food in their own garden, there is an experience of consuming food from the fruit of their labor. There is a correlation with creation in the garden of Eden when people tended to the ground, which is where the food source began.[62] "God meets people at the table."[63]

Modern statistics about mealtimes are astounding. One in four people eat at least one fast-food meal every single day. American households spend roughly the same amount per week on fast food as on groceries. According to Cody Delistraty, writer for *The Atlantic*, the majority of American families report it is rare to eat a single meal together on a regular basis.[64] There are not only financial and relational ramifications of meals eaten in

60. Willimon, *Sunday Dinner*, 10.

61. Fick, *Food, Farming, and Faith*, 8–9.

62. Ayres, *Good Food*, 2–4.

63. Ayres, *Good Food*, 54.

64. Delistraty, "Importance of Eating Together," para. 2.

vehicles, but the food that is eaten is usually less nutritious than foods cooked in a home. Homemade foods generally have lower fat, salt, and caloric content.[65]

There has been a movement within restaurants nationwide to create a space that is more like home than a fast-food restaurant. Wendy's and McDonald's restaurants have both done significant remodels to their franchisees through the years where they are creating living room environments with fireplaces and communal tables.[66] All the while, table and dishware sales are declining, because more and more people are eating takeout, premade food, and are sitting in front of screens or standing at the counter to consume their meals.[67]

Many owners are converting the tables in their restaurants, cafes, and diners into spaces that place people near one another, or seat multiple people together, even if they are strangers. This is not a new idea, as counter seating and cafeteria-style tables have been around for years.[68] The founder of Starbucks, Howard Schultz, has the desire for people to consider their Starbucks coffee shop a third space (assuming that home and work occupy the first and second location where people spend their time). He would like to welcome people by name and have them be known for their drink of choice.[69] Coffee is no longer just something that you drink. When you go to Starbucks, you have an experience.[70] Is that what people are longing for, an experience? An authentic connection with another human being is something that people ache for daily. Often people will settle for a connection at a café or coffee shop, even if the staff only know their name and their drink of choice.

Recovery of the communal identity of family around a table is needed as it is communicated in Scripture, as it is a vital formational tool for spiritual, relational, and physical nourishment.

65. Pollan, *Cooked*, 8–9.

66. Braun, "Alone Together," para. 17.

67. Fresco, "Why We Eat Together," 6.

68. Braun, "Alone Together," para. 8.

69. Schultz and Gordon, *Onward*, 13.

70. Sweet, *Gospel According to Starbucks*, 3.

Paul Fieldhouse, who has an interdisciplinary degree in food and religion, offers these insightful words, "Across cultures and time, food sharing is an almost universal medium for expressing fellowship; it embodies values of hospitality, duty, gratitude, sacrifice, and compassion. Giving, receiving, and sharing food are gestures of friendship and symbols of trust and interdependency."[71]

Cooking meals together and creating a hospitable space are primary ways to expand who is present at the table within a home. People feel welcome when there is an invitation to share a meal at someone else's house.[72] Times of celebration and loss are often when people need the hospitality offered by a meal. It is important to remember that people need others during the immediate time of joy and loss. People need tangible support: oftentimes fruits and vegetables are what is needed, the basics of life.[73]

During a season of my career working in higher education I received news of a potential job loss due to financial instability within the organization. I was devastated thinking about the potential impending loss. That very same day my friend Ethan called to connect about an upcoming meeting we had together with church. During the conversation my current work situation came up and he was gracious in offering his concern for me. A couple hours later I received a text, "We are so sorry about this potential loss. Sarah and I would like to order you dinner for carry out or delivery. Let us know what night is best and we will call it in." I remember the surprise I had hearing these words, as I thought, "People send meals when babies are born or someone close in your family dies, not for a potential job loss." I was reminded through their kind gesture that loss is loss, and having other people present in that space of offering a meal was a supportive gesture.

Support is something needed not just with beginnings and endings, it is needed in on a regular basis. The shaping that takes place around breaking bread together is formational in how memories are created. People can recount events, conversations, and

71. Fieldhouse, "Eating Together," 3.

72. Julier, *Eating Together*, 1.

73. Roberts McWilliams, "Love, Loss and Fruit Salad," 239–40.

emotions that have been experienced around a meal at the table. Tables can be a place where conflict arises as well as a place where it can experience apology.[74] The table is an altar where forgiveness, remembering, and celebration can be shared with other people. David Adamson has articulated this formational space by sharing,

> Do you know what an altar is? If I asked you to picture an altar in your mind, I bet you'd image a table at the front of a church with a Bible placed right in the middle of it, right? It's the special place where the pastor or priest stands to teach about God.
>
> But, since before the time of Jesus, Jewish Rabbis have taught that every table is an altar—every table is a place where worship happens. Every table is a place where relationships are established or repaired, a community is developed, guests are welcomed, forgiveness, and peace are extended. And it is from ordinary tables that we give thanks to God.
>
> Perhaps this is why Jesus referred to the Kingdom of God as a feast. Jesus would often eat with sinners, or cook breakfast for his followers—and each time he did, he was revealing the Kingdom of God. To this day in the Middle East, to invite someone to dinner is to extend peace and forgivingness to them, because every table is an altar where you experience God. In fact, the Hebrew word we translate as "altar" is "mizbeach" (pronounced "miz-bay-akh"), which means "to offer an animal" either as a sacrifice—or for eating. Built into the word is the idea of a meal!
>
> What I love about this idea is that at God's table, it's not just the pastor, priest or leader who is welcome—we are ALL invited.[75]

In order to proclaim the power, restoration, and hope of Jesus, the table needs to become a place where the truth of Jesus transfigures identity. "And people will come from east and west, and from north and south, and recline at the table in the kingdom of God" Luke 13:29. May people host and gather around breaking

---

74. Nouwen, *Bread for the Journey*, 18th entry.

75. Adamson, "Photo of an Open Bible."

bread together in order to embody love and belonging as image bearers of our Divine Trinitarian God.

Reflection Questions

1. Where are meaningful places that represent love and belonging in your life?

2. Throughout the Biblical narrative the altar and table have been places of gathering; have these spaces influenced your understanding of connecting with the triune God? If so, in what ways have you been shaped by the altar and table?

3. What are some of the formational stories that have taken place in your life around the table? Are there themes within these stories?

4. How can we create spaces at our tables where storytelling is encouraged, identities are built of connection and belonging, and communal spaces enact faithful love?

Part Three

Unification with the Triune God

[The] sacredness of the physical world—and the potential of the
physical world for sacredness—provides a powerful and surprising
path towards understanding the existence of God.[1]

CHRISTOPHER ALEXANDER

Teach me your way, O Lord, that I may walk in your truth;
give me an undivided heart to revere your name.

PSALM 86:11

Our Father in heaven, hallowed be your name. Your kingdom come.
Your will be done, on earth as it is in heaven. Give us this day our
daily bread. And forgive us our debts as we also have forgiven our
debtors. And do not bring us to the time of trial,
but rescue us from the evil one.

MATTHEW 6:9–13

1. Alexander, "Making the Garden," para. 1.

UNIFICATION MEANS THE PROCESS of unifying or uniting; union.[2] What is the first thing that comes to mind when the word "unification" is used? When is a time that the feeling of a unified front was present? What is necessary for experiencing unity in a relationship or decision? What do you imagine being the epitome of unity?

The term "united" is connected to nations, states, not for profit organizations, airlines, health care, churches, and household mantras. Yet how often is this lived experience among groups of people or missions of organizations? There are treaties that are in disarray among leaders, party lines are divided, and financial agreements among organizations who cannot reach consensus. Relationships are holding onto privilege, power, and pride rather than seeking restorative wholeness. Each of these scenarios are blockades to unification with the Triune God of love.

Transcendent Unity

The Hebrew word for unity is *yachad*, which means "to be united" or "to meet," and in Greek the word for unity is translated "oneness" or "unanimity."[3] The unblocked connection to oneness was the intention of the Divine Triune God. Oneness in relationship with the *Imago Dei* was the hope from the beginning. Once there was a disruption and fracture in this union, the invitation became clear that God was present and sacred spaces to gather to meet God would be the way to redeem the lost connection.

Tabernacles, temples, cathedrals, chapels, and churches are a few of the spaces people have believed to be inhabited by God. Throughout time these spaces were not limited to a building, but a symbol of a sacred space could be found at the table, an altar for people to gather to experience unification with God. The altar of the Old Testament became the table of the New Testament where unity in relationship was experienced with the Divine.

2. See "Unification."

3. Strong, *New Strong's Expanded Exhaustive Concordance of the Bible*, 89, 111.

Sacred places and sharing meals are not new concepts. Creation is a backdrop full of opportunities to acknowledge where God has been or where the wrestling with God has taken place. In the Genesis 16 account of Hagar's story, she found a place with El-roi, the name for God meaning "the one who sees." Samuel set a stone down in 1 Samuel 7 between Mizpah and Jeshanah, naming it Ebenezer, meaning "Thus the Lord has helped us." Places mark important moments and often are grounding for reflection of what has taken place.

There is a swingset in the backyard at my parent's house that reminds me of a sacred childhood moment of encountering God. A small cement prayer chapel in Indiana has been a setting for a number of conversations wrestling with the Eternal Other about the way forward. Vineyards, kitchen tables, and fire pits have also held conversations that have provided consecrated places for transformational conversations.

Spaces set aside with the intention of encountering God and others takes hopeful belief that we will encounter El-roi. Jesus took a loaf of bread at a table and broke it as a semiotic visual of the foretelling of his broken body. The cup of wine was lifted as a sign of the new covenant instituted as a practice to partake in as a form of remembering. This all happened at a meal. There continues to be an invitation to gather together regularly to encounter connection.

An experience in a space set aside with other people participating in taking communion is essential to our unification with the Trinity. Creativity can also be present perhaps by sharing coffee or brunch together after a church service, which can represents ways of participating together in unity.

After church is over, sharing a meal has been without a doubt one of my favorite times of a week for the better part of the past twenty years. For years I would host in my home at my table, which was also representational of a revolving door. Some people were present for a semester or just a few years of college, other people have come and gone because of moving for job transitions, and some were present for consecutive years. Yet Sunday after Sunday for years sharing space around a meal after church has been a way to live out the message of incarnational unity; through the discussion of the message, and sharing of communal spaces with the hope to become fertile ground for growth and enlightening moments.

There have also been seasons over the past twenty years when people who once were interested, no longer shared that same desire to gather. That is a part of being in relationship with others. Humans have free will, and it is easy to welcome until that free will means our lives are affected and people decide they no longer want to be included in sharing life together. Mutuality is important to growing in unification.

Breaking bread as sustenance over the course of a person's life will include consuming thousands of meals. People have choices to enter into this nourishing experience of unity in relationship with God and others. Or choices can be made to avoid the inevitable transitions of relationships that need people to change, grow, and consider another person in loving ways. Choosing healthy interactions can repair or repel union in relationships. Nourishment, physically and relationally, can be a way to experience union within building strong mutuality.

Nourishment and union.

These two words found new meaning as they came to life during a month spent in India in May of 2011. On this particular day we were at a home of the Missionaries of Charity founded by Mother Teresa, named Prem Dan. Upon arrival, the painted sandstone metal gates opened and the crowded bus of volunteers from all over the world exited near one of the buildings where we were greeted by the kindest Sisters of Charity. This was a home for women with mental, developmental, and physical limitations who were not welcomed into society due to the cultural caste system.

There was a distinct smell that lofted through the air, one part bleach water, one part cooking oatmeal. Both separate from one another are tolerable. Together, though, it seemed to be a bit more than my stomach could handle. During the introductions, I stepped into the restroom so that my nausea would be contained during our morning orientation. I then leaned on the sink looking in the mirror and gave myself a pep-talk, "I can do this. I can do this. I can do this." Taking in breath after breath the smell was neutralized and I was able to hear the rest of the instructions for the day.

After turning my senses outward, I became familiar with the exterior of the white cement buildings with painted murals and the kind voices of the sisters who would instruct the volunteers for the day. All were welcomed into the large room where approximately twenty five to thirty women slept, ate, and spent their days in their simple wooden chairs with wheels, resembling a wheelchair of sorts.

The bodies of the women were frail, tender, and personified the body frame of a child around the age of ten years old. In actuality the women were anywhere from twenty to thirty years of age, and had been dropped off at the gate after their birth family realized they had significant needs. Their entire lives would take place in this large room, lit with the sunlight of the day, and the shimmer of the moon would be their nightlight. None of the women could form audible words, but were communicating with their verbal squeals, cries, and expressively waving their arms. The sister in charge on this particular day would introduce the volunteers and the women would stomp their feet in unison as an expression of welcome.

There was a contagious presence of joy in the room, as everyone was together. Communication was done through stomping of feet or an occasional cry expressing hunger. Communicating with a variety of expressive cries, noises, or words are universal forms of language when it comes to being hungry.

As we put on our aprons made from material of refurbished saris, to begin feeding each woman breakfast, I remember the music in the background which seemingly meant that it was time for spoonfuls of oatmeal. Each woman sat in her chair, awaiting her turn to be fed. Each volunteer picked up three trays of oatmeal from the cafeteria counter for each of the women we would feed.

I sat down and took another deep breath.

As I positioned myself in front of the three women who I would be spoonfeeding their first meal of the day, I noticed the water pooling in the corners of my eyes. I took another deep breath. Day after day these women, many of whom were the exact same age as me, without any of their motor skills functioning at full capacity, would rely on volunteers to feed them. Each meal. Every single bite of food they would ever consume would come from the hand of another person. Each sip would be lifted to their mouth from a straw.

I took another deep breath.

With deep gratitude for the opportunity to sit with the fragility of humanity I continued to feed these three women their breakfast.

Lingering at a meal is one of my favorite things about gathering with other people. Yet this morning, the clock was ticking minute by minute, and it had nearly been an hour of feeding the women what was now cold and sticky oatmeal. They did not seem to mind, though, that it was taking a long time. Someone was with them as they squealed between bites or motioned for a drink when needed. At first I was in a hurry to finish the task, so to speak, but then after approximately fifteen minutes I realized that I needed to settle in and embrace each bite, no matter how long it would take.

After the hour had passed I was able to wipe the feeble hands and tender faces of these women as I would prepare to feed the next three women who were scheduled for their breakfasts. This cycle would take place over the next eight hours, transitioning at some point to a soup for lunch.

My emotions would play ping pong throughout the day from water-filled eyes and joy-filled glee as I watched the satisfaction of these women as they simply ate their meal. The physical needs of each of these women were tended to by the volunteers every single day of their life.

Each bite was manna for that moment, for that meal of the day.

The afternoon bells chimed, noting a break in the day. I decided to step outside to get a breath of fresh air before the snack-time would start. As I was taking off my apron to hang on the hook by the exit, I went to open the door to take my first step outside of the cement room, and the dam that was holding back my water-filled eyes let loose and tears began to roll rapidly down my cheeks.

Through the blurry stream, I noticed the entrance of the prayer chapel was directly in front of me. The doorway was wide open as if the architect knew the access to a sacred space needed to always be open for whoever needed a place to encounter the Divine Triune God.

I walked into this small cement chapel with lament over the brokenness of the bodies of these women who had been cast out of society and left orphaned. Abandoned, alone, vulnerable, and disregarded, these women were not welcome in society. I cried out loud to the good God I said I believed in and said, "Why, why, why? Why, God, must these women suffer alone with bodies that do not function on their own? Where are you God? If every human is made in your Divine Image then why is this brokenness of bodies and systems present?"

The tears continued to mix with sweat droplets rolling down my face as the afternoon heat from the sun filled the chapel as if it were a sauna.

I put my face down into my cupped hands weeping at the thought of their pain.

The bells rang a few more times with intervals of silence and temperatures of heat rising throughout the afternoon.

At one point, when the tears had slowed their roll, I looked up at the front of the church and saw a statue with hands reaching out. As I took yet another deep breath, I remember that still small voice that Scripture talks about, reciting the words of Matthew 25, "for I was hungry and you gave me food, I was thirsty and you gave me something to drink, I was a stranger and you welcomed me."

It was as if in that moment the unification with the Divine Triune God and each of us were a part of making the world whole. We each had a need. We each had our limitations. We were each in longing for nourishment. We each needed to let the tears come along with the joyful laughter. We each needed each other.

On this day, the Divine unification of the Trinity was experienced, it was as if all were well in the beginning. A trinity, a union of nourishment transcended the oatmeal trays on that day in Calcutta, India.

Genesis Account of Unity

In the very beginning, God created male and female in the image of the Creator God, Jesus, and Holy Spirit. Shortly after the creation of humankind, the gift of food became a central part of the Biblical narrative. God gave Adam and Eve permission to roam the garden and eat of all food, except for the fruit from the tree of knowledge of good and evil.[4] From this portion of Scripture, we learn that God is a communicator, there was plenty of food to eat, and there were boundaries in place. God's first communication about the food was a resounding "Yes, eat and enjoy!" As the narrative unfolds, sin enters the garden when Adam and Eve violate the boundary and eat of the fruit. From this point on throughout Scripture, God initiates relationship to experience reconciliation and continues to show up to share space together.

Even today, a meal around the table breaking bread can be a place for narratives to unfold. Each day can be full of emotions, relationships, and stories that affect the way people interpret and experience the world. Over time, these stories influence the way people see themselves, and yet who are the recipients of the communication of these experiences? Relationships are sharing less face-to-face time together because of the connectedness that happens via technology as well as less time shared together because of choices with schedules that isolate people from one another.

In addition to this, the definition of a home does not always include what people imagine as a traditional family that once seemed to be idyllic in some cultural contexts. Dad, mom, and children are not the soul definition for who makes up members of a household. The number of people who are choosing to have other expressions of relationship that do not include proximity is becoming normalized. These relational shifts are present inside and outside of the church.[5] The result of people's choices to not live in relationship with others on a consistent basis often times results in disconnection and isolation.

4. Genesis 2:17.
5. Hamaker, "Pew for One."

As disconnection is on the rise there is a severing of people sharing relationship with one another as created image bearers of the Triune God. The core identity longing within humanity is for interconnected relationships that are transfigurational. People want to be connected, known, seen, heard, and invited to share space together.

Relationships are formational as each person is created in the image of the Triune God. They offer sharpening to one another for the experience of love and redemption. In order to share life with other people, one's eyes must open to the people around oneself, extend an invitation to come to the table, and give an option to choose to participate in breaking the bread together. When this happens, it communicates the story of the gospel's redemption in a transfigurational way, as modeled by the *ecclesia* in the first century around the table, sharing life together.

Cultivating ideas is something that my friend Lauren does effortlessly, yet with generosity. She advocates for individuals in our county to be places of refuge, safety, and affordability as she works in the margins with people who are trying to find homes. She also researches and creates beautiful masterpieces, one of which is the dining room table that she built. It is large, hand-crafted, and stunning.

Our friendship, alongside her husband Mark and their children, has expanded across states and through so many shared moments of moves, relational transitions, losses, deaths, and shared hopes. The times that we have met around this table have been simple, yet often held hours of conversation.

At one point as we were talking about my deep care for the table to be a stabilizing place for people she said, "As a daily reminder for gathering people, you can build a table for your house, it is easy!" Lauren and I define "easy" differently, yet she stirred me to imagine this possibility.

A few years went by and one day I mentioned this to a few friends as I was preparing to finish up my doctoral research work on the table. One week, Nolan and Becca graciously drew up the plans with me, went to the lumberyard, and found a woodworking shop where, in the middle of winter, we could make this dining room table. The hand-drawn plans on graph paper could have been a sibling to the table that Lauren built. These drawings would become transformed into a physical manifestation of a place to gather in my home on a regular basis.

I was overcome with gratitude that at times our desires can be communal, something that can be experiential for a collective.

Shortly after the table was built I was moving to a new home and had a couple of months where I needed to put everything I owned into storage. I researched how to store this large oak table, with dark espresso-toned stain sealing in the color, and found that storing it flush against the storage unit would be best to keep weight off of the legs of the table while it was sitting in a ten by ten storage unit packed full of boxes.

Moving day often evokes a plethora of thoughts and emotions as transitions of any sort involve so many nuances. So many people graciously came to help transport my belongings to storage. On this particular February day, the table was leaning against the wall shielded by a blanket and a few people were propping it up as it was being secured to the wall, when all of a sudden I watched the table fall in what seemed to be in slow motion with the sound of wood splitting and a leg falling off as it crashed against boxes, wooden crates, and people. Once we realized that no one was physically hurt, I stood there in shock watching this metal, hairpin leg dangling back and forth from the braces on the bottom of this hand-built table. All the while my friend, Tyler assured me it could be fixed. I borrowed his confidence as we all proceeded to restack boxes until all was settled into its spot as if we were stacking pills in a game of Dr. Mario.

We put the padlock on the storage unit and I stepped into the moving truck when the tears began to well up in my eyes. My hand-built table was cracked, broken, and I did not know if it would be the same. I knew it was just a table, yet I realized it was not about the crack in the table or the leg breaking off, it was that this symbolically represented how I was experiencing communal spaces in recent years in a few of the most important relationships in my life.

My hand-carpentered table was seemingly unstable in what it could stomach, useless as it leaned up against a wall in a storage unit, unsupported as people appeared to be present, yet not watching closely the things that held so much meaning. I stared at the road with tears in my eyes, feeling disappointed and sad, as I drove back to return the moving truck.

In the weeks and months that followed, this symbolic imagery would come up in therapy, as well as in conversations, as I was sorting out my understanding of the table and if it really did hold the depth of meaning I believed. I pondered questions about the idea of the table and the intersectionality of the communion we were meant to experience on a regular basis. Was the table really a place to come together? Was the table going to actually be a place where people would love as the Trinity loved? Would the table split in such a way that it could not be restored?

All the while I was asking these questions in this time of transition, my friends Kate and Steve had extended an invitation to me to come and live with them while I was waiting for my new place to open up. During these months I had no idea that although I was making monthly payments for my broken dining room table to be bolstered up in a storage unit, unstable, useless, and unsupported, I was living in a home among a family that would be slowly rebuilding my understanding of what it meant to be present with belonging and connection.

Morning breakfasts were an open invitation to join, often a hot meal was handed to me as I was hurrying off to work. I will not forget the mornings I would find a breakfast tray outside my bathroom as I was getting ready when I had a big presentation to give that day. Kate wanted to make sure that I was well-fed and valued as she often reminded me, "You are doing important work."

There was also a heaping dose of daily persistence from Nera asking for my presence with her one-year-old vocabulary, insisting that I, also known as "Mimi," would hold her. Her way of being in the world reminded me it was okay to have needs, we all do. At dinner there were countless conversations involving the stories of her older sister, three-year-old Jace, at the table about the trickiest parts and the favorite parts of our days. And we gave up hours of our sleep, sitting at the table when the adults would process the days we had experienced once the kids were settled in their beds.

Unbeknownst to me, these months were repairing my belief that the table could be stable, necessary, and accessible. I remember a few times sitting with tears running down my face as I was sharing about a hurtful encounter with loss, work, or decisions that were being made, and Jace would come and wipe the tears from my eyes asking, "Are you sad, Mimi? It's okay to be sad, it means your heart is getting bigger."

Indeed my heart did expand in those months in ways that offered healing that could only come through incarnational love of living among relationships. Trinitarian belonging can be extended through incarnational love.

When I would leave for a weekend, I would get a video message or a call from Jace asking me when I was coming home. Being in relationship extends care that invites unifying relationship. Sharing space with people is not a work of charity or for the faint of heart. It is an extension that we all need to know that our presence is welcome. It is mutual all throughout the rhythms of the day.

One morning, Kate announced that she might have overstepped her boundary with me as she proceeded to share that upon my impending move that was coming up she had arranged with some friends for my table to be fixed by a local woodworker. I stood near the corner of the counter with my coffee in hand stunned with gratitude as I listened to her reveal the plan for the repair.

Throughout the weeks that were leading up to this move, amidst a number of logistics that had been set up for a truck, moving helpers, timing, setting up electric and water bills, an address change, and on and on, I would lay in bed thinking about seeing the splintering, cracked, and broken-legged table again and thinking about how to figure out how to fix this heavy, eighty-by-forty-inch table. I would lay there alone, knowing it was not just about the table, it was about something more.

Often "this" is really about "that."

Simultaneously I would also think about the fracturing that was taking place in relationship as friends who I had been in community with for almost two decades were consistently making decisions that were no longer holding intentionality to the inclusivity of communal dreams we had once shared together. The tables where we spent years challenging, growing, and dreaming together for a communal life were slowly cracking in ways that seemed unrepairable. I felt as if I was being taken out at the knees as I was heartbroken at this looming loss of people I love dearly.

"This" table that was splintered was also about "that" severing relationship.

We are hurt in relationship and we heal in relationship.

Moving day came again, and I watched Drew, Steve, Brad, Mason, Molly, and Max transport the broken table onto the bed of our friend Scott's truck. I sensed that I was watching a modern-day version of the New Testament story of the people lowering the lame man on his mat to meet Jesus. Sure, it is just a table, some might say, but for me it was a physical representation of what I believe to be an essential place to gather people. This broken table was going to be restored so that it could become a stable place to extend nourishment through healing, growing, dreaming, hoping, becoming, and loving others.

Although the repair work takes time and intentionality, whether it is through woodworking or relational reconstruction, I believe it is possible to experience communal love and belonging.

The table is a space where people can come together to break bread, pray, share in song, read liturgy, express lament, or tell stories with other people to strengthen their identity as image bearers of the Triune God and as a flourishing evolving *ecclesia*. The table is a space to invite transparency in being seen and known. This is a gathering place for people to come together in order to build a community of meaning and belonging. This happens through relationship with the Triune God, invitation, participation, and communication around breaking bread with one another. This is an expression of embodiment by coming together as a representation to the world of love. This then is a transfigurational experience around the table where people are welcome to belong.

This embodiment of sharing together establishes the identity of believing in the redemptive power of Jesus who can transfigure lives, offer forgiveness, and hope for those who allow redemption to be their way of life through love, healing, joy, and peace. As my parents, John and Jill, have shared from over forty years of making meals, "It is through sharing stories around the table that we really do understand how to care for each other because of God, Jesus, and the Holy Spirit. It is truly a blessing to gather together."[6] The story of love can be experienced at a table where love is the foundation and authentic care is extended.

Love is incarnational, as Augustine of Hippo has stated, "You are to be taken, blest, broken, and distributed, that the work of the Incarnation may go forward." The narrative of Scripture includes an offer to choose to be in relationship with the Triune God. Theologian Kelton Cobb writes,

> The table, the trough, has God's fingerprints all over it. We participate in a mystery whenever we eat food. Indeed, every meal is sacramental. Through eating, death is resurrected into life. Dead fish, dead figs and dead cornflakes transformed into the living tissue of our bodies. This is an event I would call a holy occurrence.[7]

YHWH is a God of provision.[8] "The Lord upholds all who are falling, and raises up all who are bowed down. The eyes of all look to you, and you give them their food in due season. You open your hand, satisfying the desire of every living thing."[9] Throughout the Old Testament, fellowship over a meal was a way of reaching out

---

6. John and Jill Hurlow, interviewed by author, Mansfield, Ohio, May 15, 2017.

7. Minich, *The Rainbow Diet: A Holistic Approach to Radiant Health through Foods and Supplements*, 78.

8. MacDonald, Ehrensperger, and Rehmann, eds., *Decisive Meals: Table Politics in Biblical Literature*, 2.

9 Psalm 145:14–16.

and bringing reconciliation.[10] The New Testament recounts that more people received an invitation to lunch from Jesus than an invitation to the synagogue.[11]

Sharing food and stories among other people are practices that span across cultural, generational, and social boundaries. A shared meal around a table at one time was a central focal point of a home and has been a place for people to share stories on a consistent basis ever since. The time spent together around breaking bread in the Scriptures, according to Professor Hal Taussig, was where

> They made decisions together about their inner workings and their relationship to the broader world. Meals can be places where people are taught, learn together, and where they worshipped, prayed, and sang their songs together. Even as toddlers, my sweet friends, Charlie and Theo, sing their meal time prayers with robust appreciation. This time can be where people have arguments, sort out differences, went their own ways, and reconciled with one another. It was a central community event. These meals provided the primary experiential evidence for those who opposed them, those who dropped in for visits, and those who were curious about them.[12]

Interconnected relationships offer a tangible reflection of the Triune God. Collective relationships bring the presence of God to life by interacting in a way that offers love, inclusion, and interdependence.

Transfigurational Image Bearers

The transfiguration of Jesus spoken of in Matthew 17:1–3, 5–8 shares that,

> Six days later, Jesus took with him Peter and James and his brother John and led them up a high mountain, by themselves. And he was transfigured before them, and

10. Webster, *Table Grace*, 11.

11. Webster, *Table Grace*, 9.

12. Taussig, *In the Beginning Was the Meal*, 21–23.

his face shone like the sun, and his clothes became dazzling white. Suddenly there appeared to them Moses and Elijah, talking with him. While he was still speaking, suddenly a bright cloud overshadowed them, and from the cloud a voice said, "This is my Son, the Beloved; with him I am well pleased; listen to him!" When the disciples heard this, they fell to the ground and were overcome by fear. But Jesus came and touched them, saying, "Get up and do not be afraid." And when they looked up, they saw no one except Jesus himself alone.

This story offers perspective of the divinity of Jesus to his close disciples. According to Don Stewart, a contributing writer for Blue Letter Bible,

> The Transfiguration was the glorification of the human body of Jesus. On this occasion His body underwent a change in form, a metamorphosis, so that it shone as brightly as the sun. At the time of the Transfiguration, Jesus' earthly ministry was coming to a close. He had acknowledged that He was the Messiah and predicted His death and resurrection. Now He was to reveal, to a select few, His divine glory.[13]

This transformation was representational of the change that is possible for the believer when one will live into the likeness of God as an image bearer of the Divine. As professor, Dr. Drew Moser, has written, "Deep transformative work requires observation, time, and reflection."[14]

Metamorphic change is possible for the Jesus follower to embody the attributes of the Triune God. Writer Jan Richardson refers to a vastness to the table when she wrote this poem entitled "Table Blessing":

---

13. Stewart, "What Was the Significance of Jesus' Transfiguration?," para. 1.
14. Moser, The Enneagram of Discernment, 35.

Transcendence at the Table

To your table
you bid us come.
You have set the places,
you have poured the wine,
and there is always room,
you say,
for one more.

And so we come.
From the streets
and from the alleys
we come.

From the deserts
and from the hills
we come.
From the ravages of poverty
and from the palaces of privilege
we come.

Running,
limping,
carried,
we come.

We are bloodied with our wars,
we are wearied with our wounds,
we carry our dead within us,
and we reckon with their ghosts.

We hold the seeds of healing,
we dream of a new creation,
we know the things
that make for peace,
and we struggle
to give them wings.

And yet, to your table
we come.
Hungering for your bread,
we come;

thirsting for your wine,
we come;
singing your song
in every language,
speaking your name
in every tongue,
in conflict and in communion,
in discord and in desire
we come,
O God of Wisdom,
we come.

May we come in whatever state we find ourselves to a table where we believe healing can come. May we find strength is being together through nourishment in ways that speak the language of unification.

All people reflect this connection and can offer tangible experiences of loving and belonging through peace-filled embodiment around a table. Paul Pastor, author and speaker, writes, "My word will not return to me without benefit, without life, without nourishing all who call me Father. I will feed you, just as I water my fields that lay full of the sprouting seeds, raising the bread of God. You will be given bread and body. You will become bread and body."[15]

A transfigurational experience around a table communicates what is necessary when it comes to teaching why gathering to break bread together is helpful to build interpersonal relationships as well as share stories of faith. In an interview with my Uncle Len, he shared the following thoughts: "What is the big significance of the 'table' that we experience? There is most likely something about that joining of all believers that will weld/meld/join us together for eternity."[16] Shared meals together around the table is foretelling for the eternal banquet feast.

15. Pastor, *Listening Day*, 46.
16. Len Calhoun, interviewed by author via email, April 5, 2017.

Places for Scriptural Storytelling on a Rhythmic Basis

A rhythm builds into the infrastructure of each day through meal-time, which is something that could be shared around a table. Jennifer Ayers, a professor and writer on faith formation and food justice, communicates the power of storytelling in a beautiful way by saying, "At the center of the Christian tradition sits a table. It was around tables that Jesus taught, loved, shared with, and challenged the disciples. At meal times, Jesus and the disciples shared a beloved community that understood sharing, hospitality, and attention to material needs to be at the heart of their life together."[17] Teaching through verbal direction as well as nonverbal modeling are important aspects of meal times around the table for children to learn the social norms of the family or those present within the home.[18] To share daily experiences and reflections around mealtime offers an opportunity for interdependence to take place, which emulates the Triune God. The prominence of the table throughout Scripture has variations of what takes place in these settings as rhythms form.

Throughout the Biblical arc, there are a variety of spaces for meals to take place for people coming together. These encounters over meals take place in order to bring God to the people and people to a more robust understanding of God. Sharing conversations of the story of God's timeless narrative are foundational. Each time there is a gathering together for a meal, there is a purpose that draws the individuals present to experience something about the Triune God. My Uncle Jim, an architect, reflects on the connections of designing church and home spaces: "There are sacred worship experiences that are established around the table, within the church building, as well as the home, both offer opportunities to share God's story of belonging."[19]

There are a number of places that people gather together with a variety of tables. It is important to recognize places can be

17. Ayres, *Good Food*, 55.

18. Fieldhouse, "Eating Together," 5.

19. Jim Calhoun, interviewed by author, Columbus, Ohio, March 4, 2016.

for different purposes of meeting. Six places as it pertains to the narrative of storytelling throughout Scripture are included in this section, *koinonia, anamnésis, deipnon, syneuōcheomai, symposium,* and *aineō.*

Koinonia

Koinonia is a place for participation, communion, and gathering. A meal is a place for fellowship together. This happens when there is participation in an effort to create opportunities to listen, challenge, and share with other people. There cannot be a separation of the bread and wine with the idea of sharing a meal together because the table is a place for telling through a Eucharistic practice which is essential to unifying believers.[20]

Where *koinonia* is present there is fellowship as a body of Christ.[21] Where there is true love for one another, the practice that emulates the *ecclesia* is present. When this is present, the incarnation of Jesus Christ offers a transfigurational experience. The unity of *koinonia* across denominational lines, economic strata, and social constructs is dependent on love.[22] People practice and understand *koinonia* in a variety of ways. For example, a deeply respected friend, Sara, shares from her experiences from years of inviting her colleagues to the table, "Unity can result from facilitating connection and intimacy through conversation."

As a mother of three boys, Rachel shares that connection can take place around the table through ongoing developmental learning while your kids are growing up. My Aunt Mary Ann allows for evolving variations of the table, by adding a leaf or setting up another table for the guests. Another perspective comes from my Aunt Molly, who has hosted holiday meals for decades, "Hosting people is really about creating opportunities—not putting on a

---

20. Welker, *What Happens in Holy Communion?*, 37.
21. Kurosaki, *One Body in Christ*, 49.
22. Kurosaki, *One Body in Christ*, 70.

performance."[23] Koinonia requires genuine intentionality to bring people together.

There is a need to put aside distractions in order to participate with the people present at the table, because as William Willimon has stated, "the disintegration of table fellowship often leads to the dissolution of the family."[24] There must be a commitment to protect the space at the table and to participate with one another in order to integrate storytelling of Scripture, to create space that is inclusive, even when people have different experiences or perspectives.

Anamnésis

A second place is *anamnésis*, which is a place for remembering. In the Jewish culture, meals are eaten weekly at Shabbat as a time to remember and retell the ancient Exodus story. These were not stories about the Jewish people from long ago, but are shared for the retelling and identification of the story of who they are from past generations to the present.[25] The table is a covenant for people to come together in mutual agreement to remember the extension of grace, and to believe in Jesus' redemptive power through communion together.[26] Matthew 18:20 explains there is something profound that takes place when people gather together around a table. "Where two or three are gathered in my name, there I am in the midst of them." If people take the time to gather in the name of the Divine trinity with the purpose of remembering whose they are, there will be an experience of God's presence in profound ways.[27]

---

23. Molly Calhoun, interviewed by author, Columbus, Ohio, May 14, 2016.

24. Willimon, *Sunday Dinner*, 107.

25. Willimon, *Sunday Dinner*, 14–16.

26. Stookey, *Eucharist*, 20–21.

27. Stookey, *Eucharist*, 20–21.

Deipnon

A third place is *deipnon*, a place for the sole purpose of eating. The food consumed is an important aspect of the story of Scripture. A typical diet consisted of a grain product, olive oil, and wine. These three items mentioned in Deuteronomy 7:13 and 11:14 were important representations of the covenantal agreement between YHWH and the Israelites.[28] The food was for nourishment but also held ritual recognition that was so very important to the culture. In addition to the types of food that made up a meal, the portions of the food were a part of the delineation of the guest's importance, and at times, social class.[29] Throughout Scripture, there was an awareness of the type of food eaten among different cultures as a sign of respect. Paul speaks of this in Romans 14 and 15, addressing the preferences of Jews and Gentiles.[30] The foods that people eat can tell a story of the Scriptural narrative of faith in an embodied way.

Syneuōcheomai

A fourth place, *syneuōcheomai*, is a place for feasting. Historically, in the ancient Near East, the king's power and authority was denoted through the royal table. "The earliest evidence for large royal feasting goes back to the third millennium BC. An inscription of Sargan of Akkad records that '5,400 men daily eat in the presence of Sargan, king of the world, the king to whom the god Enlil gave no rival.'"[31] In Esther 1:1–41, King Xerxes offers an example of great wealth and prestige through the elaborate table and the extravagant feast that he prepared for his companions and guests.

The English words for "companion" and "company" are both from Latin, defined as "Those who share bread with each other."[32] Throughout Scripture there is a sharing in the bread and wine that

---

28. Altmann and Fu, *Feasting in the Archaeology and Texts*, 187.

29. Taussig, *In the Beginning was the Meal*, 71–73.

30. Taussig, *In the Beginning was the Meal*, 72.

31. MacDonald et al., *Decisive Meals*, 7–10.

32. Stookey, *Eucharist*, 13.

brings people together. In Genesis 2, the early words that God spoke to Adam and Eve were in regards to the freedom in the garden to eat, and the entire narrative of Scripture closes in Revelation 19:9 with the finale of a feast of eternity, a grandiose banquet.

The ending of the story of the prodigal son in Luke 11:15–32 includes an elaborate celebration of the prodigal son coming home. The father holds a meal with a fattened calf in order to rejoice in the return of his wayward son. The gift of an elaborate party can be an opportunity to recognize that God is abundant in love and celebration.

Symposiums

A fifth place is a symposium for a discussion or teaching. Symposiums often have wine poured for a shared meal around a table to encourage ongoing discussion even after the consumption of the meal. Hal Taussig describes this space as "The part of the meal where most of the social interaction, community discussion, singing, and teaching occurred."[33] This space is vitally important as it welcomes a humble spirit to learn, grow, and be transformed.

People have the opportunity to share meals together as a way to extend hospitality. On a number of occasions, Martin and Kate Luthers' neighbors would share of their regular experience of dining at the Luther's home. Written accounts by Cara Strickland, who studied the life of Martin Luther, shares, "With a constant stream of visitors in his home, it's likely Martin rarely ate and drank alone. Not only was beer a constant of daily life while Martin was alive, sharing it together was a way to show hospitality to one's neighbors."[34]

Culturally speaking, symposiums were dinners, which for the majority of the time, included men from an upper echelon of society. When the early Christians would host open meals

33. Taussig, *In the Beginning was the Meal: Social Experimentation and Early Christian Identity*, 47, 74.

34. Strickland, "Hospitality by the Pint," Evangelical Lutheran Church of America, September 11, 2017, accessed September 21, 2017, https://www.livinglutheran.org/2017/09/hospitality%E2%80%85by-the-pint/.

and Eucharistic symposiums including all people from all social classes, they were functioning in society in a counter-cultural way.[35] The teaching component that accompanies a meal has profound implications as it brings people together for telling the story of God by modeling inclusion.

There is a quaint café named Symposium Coffee in the Pacific Northwest that embodies the essence of design for bringing people together for the sake of sharing. The first time I walked into one of the two coffee shops, I was just taken aback by the name and the meaning painted eloquently on the wall making clear the purpose for your visit was for discussion. Combined with the most delicious lavender latte I have had, it was a visit I will not forget. After a number of visits to the one location, years later I visited the second location with a group of learners who had the joy of sitting down with the owner. He shared with us the story of purposefully creating a space for conversation. We came to visit for a few hours and the multiple tables were set with a copious amount of food and more drink options than I could remember. The generosity was abundant, and it was only three in the afternoon; it was a happy hour.

Aineō

The final place is *aineō*, a space for worship. When Jesus was sharing meals, he was giving people an experience of the kingdom of God right in front of them as a form of worship.[36] The Eucharist is an opportunity for people to remember what Jesus has done through death and resurrection. This is a story that embodied the experience through redemption of moving from death to life. Revelation 19 portrays another image of the wedding feast in eternity.[37] The opportunity to worship together with other people tells the story that the creation of humans was in the image of

35. LaVerdiere, *Dining in the Kingdom of God: the Origins of the Eucharist According to Luke*, 16–19.

36. Ayres, *Good Food*, 62.

37. Rohr, "Mysticism."

relationship, to share life among each other as a community of believers.

As a place for worship, the local church has held spaces for meals together as a way for the congregation to share time with others. This is a time to participate in the teachings of Scripture and share space with people over a meal. The altar table where the Eucharist is shared within the church is focused on a time that calls people to celebrate the life of Christ, remember his sacrifice, and share in the communal experience of communion together. These tables, both over meals, as well as communion itself, have been spaces for the church to be reminded she has a place to host other people, while also being hosted. There are times to offer and times to receive. This worshipful church space provides examples of what it means to be intentional: to reach out and invite people to join as well as to share their stories.[38]

When people have a place to come to the table, figuratively and metaphorically, the action of contribution can be an enhancement to partaking in the daily bread. Richard Rohr writes, "Yes, you—and all of creation—are invited to sit at the divine table. You are called to consciously participate in the divine dance of loving and being loved."[39] Opportunities for people to participate at the table are present through the invitation to come. Jesus followers are of one body, for people all partake of one bread. Sharing a meal with other people is key to this process of fellowship and imitating the creation of relationship.[40] First Corinthians 10:17 reiterates this by saying, "Because there is one bread, we who are many are one body, for we all partake of the one bread."

The Table as a Space for Metamorphic Change

Jesus asked his disciples to partake in the breaking of bread and drinking of wine as a means of remembrance of the redemption that

38. Rhonda Conrad, Judy Crossman, Emily Vermilya, and Jackie White, interviewed by author, Marion, Indiana, October 21, 2015.

39. Rohr, *Divine Dance*, 22.

40. Milne, *We Belong Together*, 67.

was taking place because of his relational love. First Corinthians 11:24–25 states, "He had given thanks, he broke it and said, 'This is my body that is for you. Do this in remembrance of me.' In the same way he took the cup also, after supper, saying, 'This cup is the new covenant in my blood. Do this, as often as you drink it, in remembrance of me.'"[41] The word "Eucharist" means "thanksgiving."[42]

Remembering, thanksgiving, and celebrating are at the core of the Eucharist, as it is a way of partaking in the transfigurational act of the Triune God's loving relationship to us. Laurence Hull Stookey, a professor, shares these insightful words,

> Do this in remembrance of me. Yet when we come often enough and stay long enough, unwittingly the faithful find there a banquet whose richness and delight cannot be anticipated. The feast is intended to allure, then compel, and finally draw into true community those who share it. The wonder of this banquet—Christ's feast with the church—we now pursue, the better to enjoy it and to be nurtured, changed and emboldened by it.[43]

To understand the Eucharist, one must remember the transfigurational experience that took place through the redemption story of Jesus Christ. By taking the Eucharist; we can reenact it.[44] The past integrates into the present, to recreate the actual process. To engage in this process of breaking the bread and drinking the wine it is vital to participate in all of the embedded meaning that is within the heart and spirit by means of transfiguration by the living, present Jesus.

The table is a place where identity is offered as one can receive the gift that has been given for our redemption with Christ. To partake of the Eucharist is a means of partaking in the transformational power that the redemption holds for followers of Jesus.[45] The table is prepared: come expecting. "To actually

41. 1 Corinthians 11:24–25.
42. See "Eucharist."
43. Stookey, *Eucharist*, 12.
44. Willimon, *Sunday Dinner*, 26–27.
45. Vander Zee, *Christ, Baptism, and the Lord's Supper*, 189–91.

come and participate is to worship. In the Hebrew and Greek, this means that you are physically doing something in response to him. You are responding."[46]

As a social justice advocate, William McElvany has written so eloquently, "We belong to the common loaf and to each other. We belong to the one chalice which binds us together."[47] When practicing communion regularly, it has the opportunity to become an integral part of the way in which a community celebrates and reflects the incarnation of Jesus' life. This time spent together is a worship experience.[48]

Reflection Questions

1. In what ways does your relationship with the Triune God influence how you engage in building unity with people around the table on a daily basis?

2. In what ways do you embody unifying words and actions at the tables where you sit as a way to honor each person present?

3. Describe a time when you were at a table with people when transcendent unity was experienced with the Triune God in a meaningful way.

4. Remembering, thanksgiving, and celebrating are essential elements of the Eucharist, how can you include these experiences at your daily table?

---

46. Pastor Daniel Rife, interviewed by author, Marion, Indiana, March 15, 2017.

47. McElvaney, *Eating and Drinking at the Welcome Table*, 23.

48. Chapell, *Christ-Centered Worship*, 293.

Part Four

Invitation into a Place of Belonging

If you have come here to help me, you are wasting your time.
But if you have come because your liberation
is bound up with mine, then let us work together.[1]

LILLA WATSON

He brought me to the banqueting house and
His intention toward me was love.

SONG OF SONGS 2:4

All are welcome at the banquet and when you invite all,
then you will be blessed!

LUKE 14:12–14

INVITATION MEANS THE PROCESS of requesting presence.[2] What is the first thought that comes to mind when an invitation is read? What feelings are felt when a deadline is approaching to respond

1. Gray et al., *Indigenous Social Work Around the World*, 83.
2. See "Invitation."

to an invitation? Once an RSVP is given to an invitation, what is the next step? If you could imagine any invitation arriving in the mail, what would it be for?

Invitations given or received are vulnerable. The conception of an idea that evokes a desire to ask someone to join something is accompanied by a vulnerability of the space between the invitation and the response. There are times when an invitation to come to something does not require much thought other than looking at the calendar to see if there is a conflict to the date and time. There are other times, though, that the idea of showing up at a gathering, a party, a meal, or an event could evoke unwelcomed emotion because of who might be at the event or what might be required of you once you are there.

When I graduated from high school I remember feeling hesitant, and about thirty minutes before the party was supposed to start I said to my mom, "What happens if people do not come?" As any mom of multiple children, me being the second of three daughters, she responded, "People came to your older sister's party, I am sure they will come to yours." Something felt obligatory to her response, but nonetheless fingers were crossed that people would come. About an hour into the party, I remember the delight that I felt when I looked around and watched the people who had come interact with each other. Celebrations are meant to be shared.

To offer an invitation is to speak into existence the desire for people to join together. When I finished a milestone in my educational narrative, I shared my desire with some friends to celebrate with a trip to Northern Michigan. Celebrations are something I deeply value in honoring the lives and moments of importance for another. In my own desire to commemorate this time in my life, I spent a lot of time researching where to go camping, which places would capture the magnificent sights, and what was the most opportune time of year to go. This was a long-awaited trip full of anticipation of making meals around the fire and hiking. Yet, between the conception of the idea and the time of finalizing plans to leave for the trip, a series of significant relational structures were breaking down, and I called off the trip based on lack of mutuality in the relationships.

Desire is not always shared as we might hope.

Courage is required in the exposure of sharing an idea. It is also something to hold on to in the response or the neglect connected to fulfilling that desire when it is not shared. There are a number of invitations that are extended and consent is requested. Yet, people do not always value the same things, which can lead to disappointment when there is no agreement on an idea. Then there are times an invitation is extended to experience something that people may have not done before. This can lead to exposure of new opportunities for joy to exist. Each time it comes with vulnerability when an idea or hope is shared. An invitation externalizes what is internal.

Invitational Inclusion

Invitations for gathering have a number of different purposes; a few include: honoring decision-making, life-change celebrations, getting friends together, and saying goodbye. Whatever the event, there is importance to having a purpose, without it the time can miss the mark of its intended meaning.[3] It is necessary to have kindness, sincerity, and hospitality in the intentionality that is needed when offering an invitation for people to come together.

Holiday gatherings with my extended family over the years have included guests of all kinds including college friends, relatives from other sets of the family, and boyfriends or girlfriends. All are welcome. Even if they are a one-time guest or a frequent yearly guest, they can be assured to get a name tag, usually with an accenting sticker or printed image for that holiday.

One year in high school, one of my closest friends, Cicely, came to spend Thanksgiving with our extended family and is still a part of conversations years later as she was kindly welcomed. A few years later, a dear college friend, Richele, joined and it only took a couple

---

3. Parker, *Art of Gathering*, 1–2.

hours into the day for my uncle to kindly ask her to share with all twenty five or so of us about herself. Issac and David joined for a snowy year and delightfully enjoyed all of the traditional elements of the Christmas morning. To this day, guests who have gathered are mentioned and fond memories are shared. Friends who expand the nuclear family find belonging at shared experiences when sincere curiosity guides the formation of relationship.

A couple of the ramifications of saying "yes" to an invitation to be a guest at a Hurlow and Calhoun family gathering include being welcomed with curiosity, a guaranteed seat at the table, and if you come at Christmas, you will have gifts to open. People kindly introduce themselves, ask to greet you with a hug if you feel comfortable, and by the end of the day you will be welcomed to come back. At least, up to this point in history everyone has had an open invitation to return.

Hosting

The setting of the first gathering was hosted by the Triune God where invitations were made to enjoy and eat together. Parameters were given. Genesis 1:28 reads, "And God blessed them, and God said to them, 'Be fruitful and multiply, and replenish the earth and subdue it; and have dominion over the fish of the sea and over the birds of the air and over every living things that moves on the earth.'"

Be fruitful.

The invitation was to live among each other as well as the inhabitants of the earth to be fruitful. In the New Testament Paul wrote in Galatians 5:22–23, "The fruit of the Spirit is love, joy, peace, patience, kindness, goodness, faithfulness, gentleness, and self-control."

Fruitfulness.

The practice of living in community daily is an opportunity to bear fruit, each and every one of them on a regular basis.

Love.

Joy.

Peace.

Patience.

Kindness.

Goodness.

Faithfulness.

Gentleness.

Self-control.

Each one of these characteristics offers an invitation to experience incarnational belonging to all people. When someone receives an invitation from a host, it is easier to share space together because people know they have been included as a guest. There can be trust that the people desire for you to be present when an invitation is extended.

As Brad Klaver, a spiritual director, has written, all are welcome to receive an invitation to the table.

> Betrayer. Thief. Arrogant Ass. Unbeliever. Rebel-rouser. Addict. Self-sufficient. Doubter. Sexually marred. Self-promoter. Insecure Scaredy-Cat. Unfaithful. Political puppet. They were all there. Each of them, with feet freshly washed—their seat at the table—unquestioned, at least not by the One with sole authority to offer it.
>
> So too, yours. So too, mine.
>
> Remembrance is the antidote for anxiety. And we could all stand for a dose right about now. So today—take, eat, drink, receive, and remember.
>
> Your seat at the table has been pulled out for you—waiting. The invitation is ever and always "come, in fullness of who you are—in all the ways you wish you weren't." There is no need to clean yourself up first before—only just come. Sure, in sober gratitude. But surely not in shame. For His is a grace and a love, far reaching to the very end doing the impossible. For you. For me. Amen and Amen.[4]

When there is an invitation extended and showing up without pretense, there is a deep sense of peace that is present. I have had countless friends who have welcomed me to show up for a meal

4. Klaver, "Photo of a Leaf."

when I have not had it all together, these are tables I want to return to time and time again. These tables offer solidarity that we all desire belonging.

Spaces of Belonging

> May you listen to your longing to be free. May the frames of your belonging be large enough for the dreams of your soul. May you arise each day with a voice of blessing whispering in your heart that something good is going to happen to you. May you find a harmony between your soul and your life. May the mansion of your soul never become a haunted place. May you know the eternal longing which lives at the heart of time. May there be kindness in your gaze when you look within. May you never place walls between the light and yourself. May your angel free you from the prisons of guilt, fear, disappointment, and despair. May you allow the wild beauty of the invisible world to gather you, mind you, and embrace you in belonging.[5]

The narrative of Scripture around fruitfulness includes an invitation to have places to belong. There are many important places to explore where God and Jesus are a host, and how space can offer hospitality.

YHWH is a God who cares about places. From the beginning of time, having a space to eat has been a care of God's. Dr. Lisa Graham McMinn, a professor of sociology, writes, "Earth is a place of beauty, blessing, diversity, and delight, where all the pieces fit together into a complete whole."[6] In Genesis 2:16 it is written, "The Lord God commanded the man (and woman), 'You are free to eat from any tree in the garden.'" From then on eating has been a part of everyday life, a natural rhythm that takes place.[7] Adam and Eve could share in this daily practice together, which offers a

5. O'Donohue, *To Bless the Space between Us*, 43–44.

6. McMinn and Neff, *Walking Gently on the Earth*, 20.

7. McMinn, *To the Table*, 5.

beautiful model of including other people by extending an invitation to break bread together.

In Genesis 18, Abraham and Sarah naturally offer an invitation of hospitality to the three strangers who came to their tent. When they offered them something to drink and eat, they offered space for their guests to share a meal. As an architect, Carolyn Steel writes, "Few acts are more expressive of companionship than the shared meal. Someone with whom we share food is likely to be our friend, or well on the way to becoming one."[8] To offer kindness in friendship offers companionship. The word "companion" comes from the Latin "cum" (together) and "panis" (bread).[9] Sharing the table by breaking bread together is a means of offering space to share in the experience of companionship that emulates the Triune God here on earth.[10]

The kingdom of God here on earth can be an expression of the relational Triune God when there is shared space around a table. As an author and speaker on community living, Dustin Willis states, "Many Christians have bought into the cultural view that our homes are our personal and private fortresses. Leveraging our personal refuge for this mission of welcoming others may feel like a great cost, but it is a cost that is repaid with an abundance of superior joys. Loneliness is traded for community, comfort is surrendered for an eternal purpose, and detached apathy is left behind for a mission meaningful enough to give your life to."[11]

Loneliness is a pervasive epidemic in humanity, one that is not new to society. The need for relationship is at the very ethos of human existence as image bearers of the Triune God. When Jesus invited someone to share a meal, he was communicating his inclusion. Dustin Willis further shares, "I see you, and if I see you, then God sees you."[12] In a conversation with my dad, the question was asked, "How is sharing a meal around a table representational of

8. Steel, *Hungry City*, 212.

9. Chester, *Meal with Jesus*, 10.

10. Lemons, "Communities at the Tables," 165.

11. Willis and Clements, *Simplest Way to Change the World*, 18, 27.

12. Willis and Clements, *Simplest Way to Change the World*, 51.

the Triune God?" He responded, "It is by offering a seat, sharing together, and accepting each person who comes to the table."[13]

Accepting an invitation to come and take a seat at the table creates an opportunity to set down the other activities in order to be physically and relationally nourished. The table can be a place where hunger can initiate the desire to sit down, as our humanity reminds us that we need nutrition. This is a place where the table becomes a level playing field; all physical bodies need nourishment.

The invitation to welcome other people to share a meal around the table allows people to experience relationship, as does the Triune God. The equalizing nature of the table is that each person can take a seat around a table in order to be seen and see one another as they are in that moment. The hunger for relational nourishment is present and can be seen by another person. Expanding further on this thought, Dustin Willis states, "We are called to be the kind of people who enfold and embrace the lonely into community, recognize and include those who feel invisible, allow God to sustain us through food, and also through relationships he designed us to walk in and to share the truth to prodigal sons and daughters that their Father is looking for them."[14]

This kind of sharing is an outward expression of the *ecclesia* modeled by the early church. As Aquinata Böckmann, a professor in Germany, so beautifully shares, "In the early Christian community, the table community of Jesus with his disciples and other people found its expression in the Lord's Supper and the following agape meal (I Corinthians 11:17–34). We recall how important it was to Paul that especially in the *agape* meal social differences in the community not be seen; if this still occurred, he terms it an unworthy celebration of the Lord's Supper."[15] Breaking bread with other people has been taking place for years and bringing people together in ways that can offer nourishment for the body and soul.

There are meals throughout Scripture, from plentiful fruit in the garden of Eden to feedings for the masses to the Eucharist

---

13. John Hurlow, interviewed by author, March 28, 2017.

14. Willis and Clements, *Simplest Way to Change the World*, 54.

15. Böckmann, *Around the Monastic Table*, 187.

meal, each time there is formation around the shared table. As a Scottish biblical scholar, Nathan MacDonald, writes, "[The table] has decisive significance in the early Christ-movement. Meals are seen as *loci* of identity formation and transformation."[16]

Inviting people to the table is a way to offer love, acceptance, and hospitality. The whole narrative of Scripture is about the Triune God offering hospitality. In Genesis, God created space for Adam and Eve, and as Dustin Willis writes, "He provides everything they needed to thrive in created joy."[17] When Jesus came to earth, he went to people's homes often to share meals. Kay Warren, author and speaker, shares the insight that, on a regular basis, "Jesus was invited to parties!"[18] The invitation to welcome people to share a meal opens up opportunities for the Holy Spirit to work among people.

When people care for others in a way that identifies that the needs of another are noticed and important it is an opportunity for what Joseph Hellerman, a New Testament professor, calls "relational solidarity," a way to exhibit loving kindness.[19] When other people are hurting, take time to invite them to share, while listening to their need. Out of this place, one can give to another with love.[20] The Scriptures that invite people to show hospitality include Romans 12:13, "Contribute to the needs of the saints and seek to show hospitality;" and Hebrews 13:2 "Do not neglect to show hospitality to strangers, for by doing that some have entertained angels without knowing it." In these passages of Scripture, there is an invitation that God has given to extend the same offer to others in a way of hospitality "without complaining" as 1 Peter 4:9 clearly states. Hospitality offers love.

Paul uses hospitality, which would culturally include a meal, as a time that could represent a "sacrament of forgiveness."[21] In regards to forgiveness, Paul writes in Ephesians 4:32 "And be kind

16. MacDonald, *What Did the Ancient Israelites Eat?*, xvii.

17. Willis and Clements, *Simplest Way to Change the World*, 37.

18. Warren, *Choose Joy Devotional*, 22.

19. Hellerman, *When the Church Was a Family*, 216–17.

20. Warren, *Choose Joy Devotional*, 128–29.

21. Chester, *Meal with Jesus*, 48–49.

to one another, tenderhearted, forgiving one another, as God in Christ has forgiven you." In addition, David, the writer of Psalms, takes it one step further: when there is conflict present, prepare and share a meal together. Psalm 23:5 says, "you prepare a table before me in the presence of my enemies." This is a way to live out the blessing of offering sincere love.

Generous hospitality is meeting a need for all people around the table, it is offering love. This idea is captured in thoughts from Abby, as a university student she organized donations for the local community with the unused food from the cafeteria: "We wanted it to be a relationship; we wanted to have participation with college students as we weekly shared a meal together. We were hoping for relationship building, with people from the community, rather than looking down on people. We believe that these people have so much to teach us."[22]

An invitation to come to the table is enhanced when there is a place for belonging to occur. The poem entitled "You Are Here" by Arlita Ibach offers stunning imagery that welcomes people together right where they are in their story every time they enter the East Michigan shop. This poem is printed on the wall of The Red Dot Coffee Company.

Here . . . Today . . .
in this place with a story that is unique to you.
Each of us has a story that is unfolding,
Chapter by chapter, page by page.
The chapters are sometimes thrilling and adventurous,
Occasionally dark and difficult,
At times mundane and dull.
Perhaps, both beautiful and messy all at once.
Your story is important because you
have something to tell.
Something you've walked through,
something you've longed for,
something true.
Right now, the place you're in,

22. Abby McLaughlin, interviewed by author, Marion, Indiana, March 20, 2017.

that dot on the map, is real.
And your story matters.
So come on in.
You are welcome here!
We'll pour the coffee.
You pull up a chair, right where you are.

God and Jesus as Host

YHWH is a God who hosts. Hospitality is core to the intercon-
nectedness of the Triune God. Henri Nouwen shares, "Hospitality
is one of the richest biblical terms that can deepen and broaden our
insight in our relationships to our fellow human beings. Throughout the Bible, guests carry precious gifts with them which they are
eager to reveal to a receptive host."[23]

Russian painter Andrei Rublev, in the fifteenth century,
depicted the Old Testament story from Genesis 18 of the three
strangers who came to Abraham and Sarah: *The Hospitality of
Abraham*, or simply *The Trinity*. Richard Rohr has noted, "As icons
do, this painting attempts to point beyond itself, inviting a sense of
both the beyond and the communion that exists in our midst."[24]
Rohr continues to articulate the details of this painting through
the variation of the color palette noting there is a depth to the intentionality of the color choices.

> There are three primary colors in Rublev's icon, each
> illustrating a facet of the Holy One. Gold: "the Father"—
> perfection, fullness, wholeness, the ultimate Source;
> blue: "the Incarnate Christ"—both sea and sky mirroring
> one another (In the icon, Christ wears blue and holds
> up two fingers, telling us he has put spirit and matter,
> divinity and humanity, together within himself. The blue
> of creation is brilliantly undergirded with the necessary
> red of suffering). Finally green: "the Spirit"—the divine

23. Nouwen, *Show Me the Way*, 25.

24. Rohr, *Divine Dance*, 29–30.

photosynthesis that grows everything from within by transforming light into itself.

The icon shows the Holy One in the form of three, eating and drinking, in infinite hospitality and utter enjoyment between themselves. If we take the depiction of God in *The Trinity* seriously, we have to say, "In the beginning was the Relationship." The gaze between the Three shows the deep respect between them as they all share from a common bowl. Notice the Spirit's hand points toward the open and fourth place at the table. Is the Holy Spirit inviting, offering, and clearing space? I think so! And if so, for what, and for whom?

At the front of the table there appears to be a little rectangular hole. Most people pass right over it, but some art historians believe the remaining glue on the original icon indicates that there was perhaps once a mirror glued to the front of the table. It is stunning when you think about it—there was room at this table for a fourth. The observer. You![25]

Jesus models hospitality throughout the New Testament as he sits at the table with others and invites people to join. He cares for the disciples, welcomes friends, and invites people who carry pain, are ill, and are living in sin. Jesus would welcome people to the table and wash their feet as a symbolic way of love. For Jesus, holiness was less about tablets of instructions and more about common tables. Jesus did not just heal the lepers; he ate with them, and touched them. Jesus did not just raise the dead; he ate with them and touched them. Jesus did not just come close to the hemorrhaging woman; he touched her and channeled his healing strength to her. Jesus did not just love prostitutes; he ate with them and stood up for their dignity.[26]

In the Jewish tradition, intentionality is a part of the daily hospitality.[27] In that culture it was a responsibility to offer hospitality as protection to others. To provide food, shelter, and protection

25. Rohr, *Divine Dance*, 29–30.

26. Sweet, *Nudge*, 180.

27. Rabbi David Wirtschafter, interviewed by author, Lexington, Kentucky, October 12, 2015.

was a way of showing partnership with others. This place of provision is an act of mercy.[28] Hosts see the spoken and unspoken needs of the guests and seek to provide extraordinary hospitality. May the prayer of Mabel Boggs Sweet be ever true to the way people are welcomed to the table, "O Lord, let me not yearn for power seats or judgment seats but for the towel of washing feet."[29]

Space Created to Offer Hospitality

A hospitable space offers sincerity of love by saying over and over again, "You are welcome here." Historians Wilford McClay and Ted McAllister have written, "A firmer sense of place, in short, may be an essential basis for our human freedom, and the necessary grounding for a great many other human goods. They need to find some 'there' that can become an enduring 'here' for them."[30] There must be a welcoming presence in order to experience hospitality with others. A person cannot be selfish and be hospitable at the same time; the two cannot coexist. To sit down at a table that is selflessly hospitable is to have ease in a space. There is not pretense, there is presence.

People are stewards of the space God has provided.[31] Steve Clapp, a food advocate, shares this insight: "Hospitality is the attitude and practice of providing the atmosphere and opportunities, however risky, in which strangers are free to become friends, thereby feeling accepted, included, and loved. The relationship thus opens up the possibility for eventual communion among the host, the stranger, and God."[32]

In college, our friends would gather at long rectangle tables for meals that would last for hours. People would come and go during mealtimes and yet we always knew people would linger in

28. Hershberger, *Christian View of Hospitality*, 18.

29. Sweet, *Mother Tongue*, 12.

30. McClay and McAllister, eds., *Why Place Matters: Geography, Identity, and Civic Life in Modern America*, 9.

31. Milne, *We Belong Together: The Meaning of Fellowship*, 85–88.

32. Clapp and Bernhard, *Hospitality: Life Without Fear*, 31.

this space. Friends of friends would come to sit with us at the table that often felt like a train where people were consistently coming and going. There are life long relationships that formed in this space that existed with the motto, "there is room for one more." Welcoming people to come have a seat and stay a while at the table offered depth to relationships.

Throughout Scripture the recognition of love and hospitality are central themes. Romans 12:9–13 articulates this by saying, "Let love be genuine; hate what is evil, hold fast to what is good; love one another with mutual affection; outdo one another in showing honor. Do not lag in zeal, be ardent in spirit, serve the Lord. Rejoice in hope, be patient in suffering, persevere in prayer. Contribute to the needs of the saints; extend hospitality to strangers." Dietrich Bonhoeffer has written, "We must be ready to allow ourselves to be interrupted by God. It is part of the discipline of humility that we must not spare our hand where it can perform a service and that we do not assume our schedule is our own to manage, we allow it to be arranged by God."[33]

The Greek word that articulates hospitality is *philoxenia*. The word can be broken down into *philo*, which is one of the four Greek words for love, and *xenia*, for "stranger." The Greek translation for hospitality is "the love of a stranger."[34] To recognize the gift of offering space for a stranger is to extend hospitality which involves being a good neighbor.[35] C. S. Lewis shares the idea of hospitality being a space for sacramental love by writing, "There are no ordinary people. You have never talked to a mere mortal . . . next to the Blessed Sacrament itself, your neighbor is the holiest object presented to your senses."[36] To extend love to another through hospitality embodies the image of the Triune God.

There can be transformation that takes place through hospitality. Steve Clapp shares, "True hospitality is rooted in the spiritual

33. Bonhoeffer, *Life Together: A Discussion of Christian Fellowship*, 99.

34. Taylor, *An Altar in the World: a Geography of Faith, rep. ed.*, 96.

35. McMinn, *Contented Soul*, 152.

36. Lewis, *Weight of Glory and Other Addresses*, 19.

life and transforms the way we view ourselves, other people and God."[37] Tim Chester, a pastor in England, further shares,

> Hospitality involves welcoming, creating space, listening, paying attention, and providing. Meals slow things down. Some of us do not like that. We like to get things done. But meals force you to be people oriented instead of task oriented. Meals bring you close. You see people in life, as they are. You connect and communicate. It is not always easy—it involves people invading your space or going to places where you don't feel comfortable.[38]

Sharing space at the table can be unpredictable. Food can end up on the floor. Unbridled words can become messier than a food fight in the elementary school cafeteria. Yet, space to explore what is uncharted territory can also become fertile ground for growth. Growth in relationship can be beneficial when people believe that we need one another in the transformation process.

As a spiritual leader in the church, Peter Leithart shares, "We don't welcome the naked so they can be naked in our presence; we don't show hospitality to the hungry so they can watch us eat. We welcome the naked and the hungry to change their circumstances. We make room for them so we can clothe and feed them. [Hospitality] is universal welcome for the sake of renewal. We make room not to tolerate, but to transform."[39] The basic needs people have can be met through loving hospitality around a table. The primary needs of food and water are a human form of our vulnerability. Sharing space around a table also involves a level of exposure to our most intimate desires to connect, celebrate, and weep with others. In sharing space together around a table vulnerability meets vulnerability and intimacy can be experienced.[40]

When there is mutual dwelling, there is an opportunity to see another person as a place where you are safe to dwell, which

37. Clapp and Bernhard, *Hospitality*, 35.
38. Chester, *Meal with Jesus*, 15–16, 47.
39. Leithart, *Blessed Are the Hungry*, 110.
40. Nouwen, *Bread for the Journey*, 15.

then speaks, "I am his; he is mine."[41] As a leader among university students, Scott with humility has shared this blessing for experiences around a table,

> My hope is that you have moments to practice being both host and guest. That you have the chance to welcome a stranger or a friend to the table and to let them be who they are without the expectation of something different. The hope is that you have the chance to be welcomed in the same way and that you will continue to offer hospitality, I am hopeful that you will continue to seek opportunities to live out values of hospitality.[42]

Xenia: Whom to Invite?

Xenia "is the ancient Greek concept of hospitality, the generosity and courtesy shown to those who are far from home and/or associates of the person bestowing guest-friendship."[43] Offering hospitality through social bonding is an opportunity to encourage and celebrate with other people around a meal.[44] The destruction of communal hospitality will happen to people if there is force, rather than conditions in which one can freely develop and discover ways that lead to redemption in the hope to create a harvest.[45]

The table can be a representation of a place where things are as they should be, meaning that they are in a place where hope lives out among others; living as Jesus lived with others.[46] It is virtually impossible to eat a meal with others when love and inclusion are present and not feel as if you have received a blessing; the depth of

---

41. Nouwen, *Bread for the Journey*, 103.

42. Dr. Scott Barrett, interviewed by author, Upland, Indiana, May 16, 2017.

43. See "Xenia the Ancient Greek Concept of Hospitality."

44. Smith and Taussig, *Meals in the Early Christian World*, 31.

45. Nouwen, *Creative Ministry*, 81.

46. Lemons, "Communities at the Tables," 161.

a bond that can come from sharing stories together that can create a shared narrative of love.

Xenia is care with the intent of extending love and care for the stranger, friend, family member, or neighbor. Dr. Christine Pohl, a leading hospitality researcher writes, "Part of hospitality includes recognizing and valuing the stranger or guest."[47] It is clear throughout Scripture that God and Jesus did not have limitations to whom they would include in sharing a meal. As Derrek Lemons, a religion professor at University of Georgia, shares, "Jesus used the context of a meal purposefully to encourage the invited guests to consider the uninvited guests and redistribute God's blessing to the fringes of society within communitas. Communitas results as Christians share their pilgrimage with others."[48]

It was late November when we headed to Washington DC to see Yo-Yo Ma in concert at the National Cathedral. At the time, Amy was a fairly new friend, yet she had this brilliant idea to take a long weekend away in the city. Amy arranged with her friends Tamara and Derek to host us for the few days we were in the city. Although I had not yet met these people, they opened their home with bountiful gifts, maps, tickets for public transportation, and shared meals with us at their favorite restaurants. With profound attention to detail we were hosted as honored guests. Our collective friendship has now become deeply rooted in generosity even though miles separate our lives.

As Douglas Webster says, "Jesus was willing to meet people where they were in their lives because this was what it looked like to live an unbiased life of who came to the table. This was staying True to the Gospel."[49] Revelation 3:20 shares, "Listen! I am standing at the door, knocking; if you hear my voice and open the door, I will come in to you and eat with you, and you with me." The invitation of other people intends to provide a place of belonging where meaning establishes transfigurational experiences around the table, breaking bread together.

47. Pohl, *Making Room*, 31.
48. Lemons, "Communities at the Tables," 158 and 163.
49. Webster, *Table Grace*, 113.

At the Table

There's a feast set before us
A table that's filled with the riches and wealth of a King
And though undeserving,
His welcome receive
Let your soul be refreshed and redeemed
It's a table that feeds every longing
Where water will quench thirsty souls
Come tattered and torn with your shame, your scorn
There will always be room for one more
At the table
There's a feast set before us
Our famine to end, let us praise the good Giver of all
He calls to us gently, His bounty to share
Oh drink deep of the cup He extends
It's a table that feeds those who look to the King
For acceptance, forgiveness, and joy
No matter your crime, there's no difference you'll find
There will always be room for one more
At the table
Brothers and sisters, all called to come
From each nation, each tribe, and each tongue
You are His guest of honor
His friend to receive
The goodness of Jesus our Lord
So lay down your hate and your neighbor embrace
Let your differences be cast aside
Let the balm of His cup reunite you in love
Cause there'll always be room for one more
At the table
He's a Savior who sees every tear when we grieve
And His blood can cleanse dirty souls
Mercy and grace
Offered free in this place
And there'll always be room for one more
He's a Savior who pleads, come sit at my feet
In my presence, you are made whole
So sit down, stay a while
You've been called, you're my child

And there'll always be room for one more . . . and one more
At the table
There's a Savior before us
The Lamb who was slain
For our pardon so we might be free
To come to the table
Come to Christ's table[50]

Reflection Questions

1. Describe a time you received an invitation to join a table where you experienced generous hospitality?

2. In what ways do you experience the Triune God as invitational?

3. What hinders you from extending an invitation to come break bread together at your table?

4. To which people outside of your nuclear family would you like to extend generous hospitality?

---

50. Vermilya, "At the Table."

Part Five

Participation in the Faith Narrative

Hospitality means primarily the creation of a free space where
the stranger can enter and become a friend instead of an enemy.
Hospitality is not to change people but to offer them space where
change can take place. It is not to bring men and women over to our
side, but to offer freedom not disturbed by dividing lines . . .
The paradox of hospitality is that it wants to create emptiness,
not a fearful emptiness, but a friendly emptiness where strangers
can enter and discover themselves as created free; free to sing their
own songs, speak their own languages, dance their own dances; free
also to leave and follow their own vocations. Hospitality is not a
subtle invitation to adore the lifestyle of the host,
but the gift of a chance for the guest to find his own.[1]

HENRI NOUWEN

"Bring me a morsel of bread in your hand." But she said, "As the Lord
your God lives, I have nothing baked, only a handful of meal in a
jar, and a little oil in a jug; I am now gathering a couple of sticks, so
that I may go home and prepare it for myself and my son, that we

---

1. Boyce, *An Improbable Feast: The Surprising Dynamic of Hospitality at the
Heart of Multifaith Chaplaincy*, 83.

may eat it, and die." Elijah said to her, "Do not be afraid; go and do as you have said; but first make me a little cake of it and bring it to me, and afterwards make something for yourself and your son. For thus says the Lord the God of Israel: The jar of meal will not be emptied and the jug of oil will not fail until the day that the Lord sends rain on the earth." She went and did as Elijah said, so that she as well as he and her household ate for many days. The jar of meal was not emptied, neither did the jug of oil fail, according to the word of the Lord that he spoke by Elijah.

1 KINGS 17:11–16

Let love be genuine; hate what is evil, hold fast to what is good; love one another with mutual affection; outdo one another in showing honor. Do not lag in zeal, be ardent in spirit, and serve the Lord. Rejoice in hope, be patient in suffering, persevere in prayer. Contribute to the needs of the saints; extend hospitality to strangers.

ROMANS 12:9–13

PARTICIPATION MEANS "THE ACT of taking part, as in some action or attempt."[2] When the host asks each person who is coming to a meal to bring something to share, what is the first thought for your contribution? What feelings are present when there are exact instructions given as to what to bring to share at a party? If someone would offer an invitation to come to a meal at the last minute, what would the go-to item be to bring? Who do you imagine will bring something creative to share?

Familiarity can be present in gatherings when they are structured, the same people are present, and recipes are made regularly to please the crowd. Yet, if the vision is lacking for why people are coming together, it is just people eating food. Inviting people to participate by bringing their flare to a meal will create a unique

2. See "Participation."

sense of representation. If an open-minded posture is present with participation, then delicacies and perfected savory dishes from the chefs among the community can be savored, even if they are not the regular menu.

Communities of people often prepare the all-time favorites, whether it is the ingredients for a themed party drink, perhaps it is as simple as brown-butter popcorn, or roasted vegetables, or freshly pressed apple cider, or queso and pico de gallo, or buttermilk oatmeal pancakes, or gluten-free chocolate cake with sea salt, or homemade scones with whipped cream, or fontina dip with homemade bread, or fried chicken, or roasted curry cauliflower.

Yet, not everyone who is invited to attend a meal is a chef. The intimidation surrounding creating a five-star dish is not a skill for all who receive an invitation. It is important to remember that people may not have the same exposure to food preparation or even a liking to the nuances of the kitchen. Welcoming environments create space for participation to be organic and unique to personal preferences.

The purpose of intentional community is to transcend the mundane elements of just eating, to sharing space with other people who bear the *Imago Dei*. The elements that nourish can be enjoyable because they are shared; whether from a recipe from someone's great grandparent that was passed down through the generations or a recipe from a neighbor or a carry-out dish from a local restaurant. The invitation for involvement embodies individuals sharing together to design the meal. This is the focal point.

Participation can be a great equalizer to financial welfare, relational status, and cooking talent. My long time friend Kristin is a part of a community in the southwestern United States which has been sharing a meal together on a weekly basis for quite some time. The people who make up this community have histories quite different from one another, whether being from a mid-America farm or raised native to New York City. Some are single, married, dating, mothers, fathers, or would like to be parents; they might be divorced or widowed. Some have criminal histories. Some have obtained degrees in higher education. Some were bathed in the

Ten Commandments as a child. Others are not sure of the order of the books in the Bible. Some have debt from homes others have debt from substances. Their lives could not be more varied.

However, the essential ingredients of this community are that everyone is invited to join and participate wherever they find themselves that week in bringing something to share with their weekly meal of rice and beans. The meal costs under five dollars to feed approximately fifteen people. Everyone has the opportunity to host the main elements of the meal as its affordability offers equality. "Bring whatever you want to add to the rice and beans" is the tag line for dinner. The additional items have included everything from hot sauce to flavored bags of potato chips to a box of pre-packaged desserts. Involvement is a contribution per each person's preference as a way of symbolizing belonging in the community.

What if this kind invitation was what more shared tables looked like? What if churches, temples, cathedrals, and community gatherings welcomed people to participate right where they were? If being inclusive, honest, and gracious were foundational around the table, how would the desire to be involved change? What if the fruitful ingredients of love, joy, peace, and patience were spoken around the table? What is there was kindness, goodness, and faithfulness when it came to how people were treated when they made mistakes? What if gentleness and self-control were marinated in people's mouths before their words left their lips? Around the table, if people came with these items on the menu, the montage of individuals would be blessed with mutuality and respect.

Yet, how often does showing up to share a meal come with unspoken expectations, passive-aggressive comments, and conflict-avoidant personalities? What benefit does gossip, arrogance, self-centeredness, or pride offer to the time together? These subtleties will spoil the environment over time, leaving people feeling segregated from participating.

When was the last time you were at a table for a meal and were alone? Alone at a table full of people. When you looked around the table and thought, does anyone notice I am here? Does anyone realize that the conversation is excluding people who are here? People might come to a share a meal together, yet relationally there are a number of layers of status present and unless there is intentionality to have impactful interactions it does not mean people are connected.

Communication and connection are vital to participation that offers a flow among people seated together. When a person is invited to show up to break bread together without a subset of unspoken or spoken obligations, interplay and ease are much more likely.

The actions of participation around a meal expound beyond words and contributions; they can include, but are not limited to, finding a recipe, buying the ingredients, bringing a dish to pass, offering a beverage, sharing a host or hostess gift, setting the dishes on the table, or pulling out the chair for another. Furthermore, taking a seat at the table and showing up with your full self is participation. Offering a blessing, prayer, or song before passing the food, helping to dish out the food, cutting up the food for one who need assistance, or offering to refill beverage glasses throughout the meal is participation.

Once there is a conclusion to the meal, engaging in the clean-up process is also participation. All of these ways of participation allow a person to engage in the experiential act of what is needed to take place in order to break bread alongside another person. This is a way to offer companionship. This is the way modeled by Jesus—he often sat down and ate with other people, thus giving Jesus the name "friend."[3]

Jesus Followers as Image Bearers of Participation

People have the capacity to participate and be involved in the formation of what happens on earth.[4] In the Genesis poem, the creation of human beings came with the opportunity to be fruitful, multiply, tend, and care for the earth within the context of the enjoying the garden. Guidelines were given to Adam and Eve to eat within the

---

3. Smith and Taussig, *Meals in the Early Christian World*, 31.

4. Chester, *Meal with Jesus*, 122–23.

garden; except for the tree of knowledge of good and evil. After deciding to forego the instructions when tempted, there was a separation that took place in relationship; yet God sent Jesus to earth to be among humankind to bring redemption and restoration.

Jesus came to live among people, to be fully Divine and fully human. He came to be in relationship with humankind, at the same time, he was in relationship with God and the Holy Spirit. He came to earth to bring redemption through his death on the cross and resurrection, which would offer redemption for the separation that choices of engaging in temptation created in Genesis. On the night before Jesus died, at the Last Supper, Jesus shared space around a table with his disciples by breaking bread and pouring wine as a remembrance of his body and blood poured out on behalf of the sins of the world, thus marking the first communion.

The broken bread and poured-out wine was a metaphoric tool as a way for Jesus to model what it would look like for Jesus followers to remember their own story of redemption and to be in relationship with their image bearer, the Triune God. The words of 1 Corinthians 10:16 are as follows: "The cup of blessing that we bless, is it not a participation in the blood of Christ? The bread that we break, is it not a participation in the body of Christ?" These questions offer opportunity for reflection as to what it means to participate in the drinking of the cup and breaking the bread.

Communal Spaces at a Table Strengthen Storytelling

To welcome people into a space and offer people something to eat is an opportunity to experience transformation. Jesus followers are anointed by the Holy Spirit, willing to live their lives as faithful image bearers of the Triune God and live lovingly with their neighbors. Demonstrating this way of living, the *ecclesia* of the early church was a place for belonging guided by the Holy Spirit, recognizing their faith was communal and offered inclusion as a form of sharing a familial identity. All of this was for the purpose of telling the redemption story of unification while breaking bread around the table. Dr. Jonathan Gottschall, an English professor, describes storytelling by writing:

> We tell some of the best stories to ourselves. Scientists have discovered that the memories we use to form our own life stories are boldly fictionalized. And social psychologists point out that when we meet a friend, our conversation mostly consists of an exchange of gossipy stories. We ask our friend 'What's up?' or 'What's new?' and we begin to narrate our lives to one another, trading tales back and forth over cups of coffee or bottles of beer, unconsciously shaping and embellishing to make the tales hum. And every night, we reconvene with our loved ones at the dinner table to share the small comedies and tragedies of our day.[5]

A commonality throughout many religious sects is that people regularly come together around a table as a way of sharing their beliefs. The sharing of faith, religion, and beliefs can take place within spiritual communities, congregations, tribes, groups, and sects in a variety of locations such as a temple, church, mosque, or synagogue. A table transcends differences, it is a gathering place for anyone to come, articulate, share, and engage in conversations of religious philosophies, beliefs, and stories that contribute to identity formation. If the table is a place of conversing about sacred beliefs there are foundational elements to the storytelling practice of passing on the religious tales to the next generation.

The presentation, preparation of recipes, and taste of food are all aspects of the table hospitality. These components are elements of hosting meals around the table in order to engage in stories of one another. These stories can take place around the meal preparation as well as the act of eating at the table. These stories include those of losses and joys, processing as well as readings, recipes, and questions to ask around this topic of bringing people together.[6]

When people come together around a table it can be for a variety of reasons: holidays or other celebratory reasons, each

---

5. Gottschall, *Storytelling Animal*, 18.
6. Gottschall, *Storytelling Animal*, 12–16.

offering an opportunity to make memories.[7] People will inevitably remember old stories, but will also create new ones through shared experiences around the table.

The rhythm of meeting once a week for a teaching, group discussion, preaching, and lifestyle practices, often are the means by which information is communicated when it comes to religious education. The communication can take place in many different variations, but each time there is an essential message communicated with the purpose of encouraging interpersonal growth with a deity.[8] The importance of understanding the robust heritage of a person's religious beliefs is a process of learning that will create depth, which will affect the family and communal narrative of sharing stories to enhance the development of faith identity. Communication is an important aspect to building relationships.[9] In order to converse around a meal, the table can offer a stage for sharing stories.

There are strong integrated narratives that come from communal experiences at a table where bread is broken and enjoyed together. When people have a space to come and sit together at a table, share a meal, along with communicating their thoughts with one another, they are embodying the relational essence of their religious narrative. A table is a gathering space for faith identity to develop, ask questions, experience exploration, and share stories.

The belonging of the early church experience happened through participation around breaking bread with other people. The participation around the table takes place through partaking in the nourishment of the bread with other people. The building of strong communal spaces takes form through the welcomed invitation to participate.

---

7. Gottschall, *Storytelling Animal*, 107.

8. Fowler et al., *World Religions*, 1–6.

9. Wood, *Interpersonal Communication*, 11–15.

Breaking of Bread by Partaking of Nourishment

"For as the rain and the snow come down from heaven, and do not return there until they have watered the earth, making it bring forth and sprout, giving seed to the sower and bread to the eater, so shall my word be that goes out from my mouth; it shall not return to me empty" (Isaiah 55:10–11). From a physical standpoint, food is replenishment for the body. The spiritual life needs nourishment as well. As Jesus followers, there is belief in a connection that symbolically takes place when people involve themselves in the Eucharist on a regular basis. Therefore, there needs to be more emphasis spent on time sharing daily meals with one another in order to consume the communal nourishment of being together.[10]

The food that is on the table becomes muscles, tissues, and bones, while the food of the Eucharist incorporates us into the body of Christ.[11] Shannon Jung, a theology professor, shares this meaningful thought, "Food is itself a means of revelation; when we eat together we taste the goodness of God."[12] There are nourishment opportunities with food that can be a part of telling the story of how God is our daily bread.

Around a table people can experience one of the most intimate places of communication that food is needed for nourishment and people are created to share space with others for relational nourishment for communion. People invite others to share space as a way to experience mutual relational nourishment. As Henri Nouwen has written, "We desire communion. That is why a refusal to eat and drink what a host offers is so offensive. It feels like a rejection of an invitation to intimacy. Strange as it may sound, the table is the place where we want to become food for one another." [13] Each meal can be an opportunity to be nourished physically and communally.

The need for food is universal throughout Scripture—whether kings, queens, or peasants, there is still hunger spoken of as a

10. Ayres, *Good Food*, 4.

11. Groppe, *Eating and Drinking*, 1.

12. Jung, *Food for Life*, 81.

13. Nouwen, *Bread for the Journey*, 1.

need. The satisfaction of food at times came through grandiose banquets; other times it was manna, each time hunger was satisfied.[14] People need food to stay alive. The opportunity to share space around a table, as well as meals, is a tangible expression of the extension of the image bearers that humans are of the Triune God. William Willimon captures this thought by writing, "In all those Sunday dinners, family night suppers, Lord's Suppers, church picnics, pancake breakfasts, barbecues, and all the rest, I learned how close our God is to us."[15]

Incorporating the Eucharist in an incarnational way, on a regular basis around a table, is helpful for people to connect their faith to what takes place inside and outside of the church. As a worship pastor at a local church, Jordan Rife, shares, "Christ has fed you, now go, and feed the world that you are actively involved in! Transformation over time, it is over a lifetime we can become holy. Partaking in communion is a part of that process."[16]

Reflection Questions

1. In what ways is it natural for you to participate at the table?

2. What keeps you from participating at the table?

3. In what ways can you emulate the posture Jesus took as it pertains to gathering around breaking bread together?

4. What can Jesus followers today learn from the *ecclesia* in the New Testament? How did people interact with one another similarly? Differently?

14. MacDonald, *What Did the Ancient Israelites Eat?*, xvi–xvii.

15. Willimon, *Sunday Dinner*, 11.

16. Pastors Jordan and Daniel Rife, interviewed by author, Marion, Indiana, March 15, 2017.

Part Six

Communication in a Community of Belonging

Words create worlds.[1]

ABRAHAM JOSHUA HESCHEL

Pleasant words are like a honeycomb, sweetness to the soul and
health to the body.

PROVERBS 16:24

So then, putting away falsehood, let all of us speak the truth to our
neighbors, for we are members of one another.

EPHESIANS 4:25

COMMUNICATION MEANS "THE IMPARTING or interchange of
thoughts, opinions, or information by speech, writing, or signs.
Something imparted, interchanged, or transmitted.[2] What feelings are evoked when truthful words are spoken kindly? What

1. Heschel, *Moral Grandeur and Spiritual Audacity*, viii.
2. See "Communication."

thoughts go through your mind when a conflicted idea is present in conversation? What do you do when someone is silent when hurtful words are spoken in your presence? When do you imagine communication being the most beneficial?

Words have the power to soothe. Words have the ability to burn. Words can be timely. Words withheld can deeply wound. Words can be inclusive. Words can challenge growth. Words can build intimacy. Words can break trust. Words can ask for forgiveness. Words can be reiterated by actions.

Words are the means to apologize and forgive. Conflict, joy, sorrow, celebration, lament, and kindness are all spoken through words. The formation of sentences and paragraphs with other people can hold ingredients that one can savor or detest. The conversation around a table can invite people to linger and continue to communicate or walk away in anger and disgust. Or perhaps you have been at a table when silence was screaming.

As I think about the times in my life when I have wanted to stay present at the table it has, at times, been because it was easy, lighthearted, and whimsical in nature. The enjoyment of each other's company was present, inclusion of thought was welcomed, disagreements were met with curiosity rather than avoidance, and the conversation transcended a timeframe.

Something seemed simple in these moments as I think about some of the most formative conversations that have taken place savoring homemade chai, drinking coffee from a machine at a gas station, or sitting at a coffee shop with toffee nut lattes eating dark chocolate. These moments have often held space for ideas to wonder, allowed for unscripted discussions, and encouraged pondering mysteries as if a mother holds a newborn baby for the first time. Time stands still and everything that was once chaotic is suddenly at peace.

Yet, there are times when some of the fiercest places of hurt, anger, or silence have been experienced around the table: the words I have not filtered through, or the hurtful things spoken that are heaped on the table have been wounding, exclusive, and isolating. Other times, when I have been on the receiving end of someone's silence, when they have chosen not to speak up or share with vulnerability, I have seen and experienced the pain from the receiving end. These are moments that slice through a relationship with the dullest of knives. At times the severing has needed time to heal. I grieve the times that relationships have been unfruitful, resulting in pruning because of toxicity.

Scripture talks about iron as a way of sharpening another piece of iron in Proverbs. I have heard people say this verse in a cheeky way to hide behind hard things that need to be said, yet it is actually a tedious necessity to be sharpened. A sharp knife is much more effective because it is precise. Relationships can offer perspectives that can differ at times, yet create necessary sharpening.

Friction is, at times, a part of communication. Salt, yeast, and oil are used as imagery in Scripture as ingredients that enhance the formation of the bread. Just as the kneading process creates necessary pressure for the dough to form, so can our words be essential for growth in relationship.

Relationship must be mutual for this kind of kneading to take place. Whether people approach communication with positivity, forward thinking, or with a reflective nature, there is a need for a variety of perspectives and experiences. The willingness to show up at the table with honesty, transparency, and vulnerability will create an environment where goodness can come from words spoken in love.

Spoken words can be as sweet as honey or as bitter as vinegar. Communication in relationships can be an incarnational representation of the Trinity when honey is applied. Yet, if people are not willing to engage in the hurt that intentionally or unintentionally is experienced, bitterness often results. This is when I have found that the feeling of invisibility lingers like the burn from hot soup on the tip of my tongue.

I have found it to be very challenging at times to understand the pain that is present within communication, or lack of it in relationships. Any time when a person's dignity has been jeopardized by another, it is hurtful. It matters every single time. It is an injustice when someone experiences abuse, exclusion, discrimination, or disregard. Sometimes pain in relationship is when people do not see eye to eye on something and, one or both people, allow those differences to create separation, rather than an opportunity to have viewpoints expanded. There can be hurt in relationship because of something destructive someone has said without remorse. There can be hurt when something has been left unsaid. We experience the pain in grief of losing someone we love over words spoken or those that never surfaced. Communication can be hurtful and can leave brokenness in relationships.

Brokenness in relationship was written about in the early writings of Genesis, as Adam and Eve chose to disregard the communication of the Creator God and ate from the tree. Yet, in the act of disobedience, God used communication to restore relationship and went towards humanity, even after being betrayed. God, in Genesis 3, sees that Adam and Eve are hiding, and God asks, "Where are you?"

Where are you? Where are you in your pain as it pertains to those people who have hurt you in words spoken in relationship? What do you find yourself hoping for in your relationships that have been severed by your own words of hurt or those of another person?

In the places where we do not understand, may there be freedom to wrestle as Jacob did to hear God's voice. It was in the wrestling that Jacob received the name Israel, which translates, "a people who have overcome." May the communication be that which allows people to overcome and build into strong relationships of love and belonging.

To be explicitly clear, I do not believe pain is God's original idea. I do not want to justify or make excuses for your pain. Your hurt matters. You deserve to be seen in your pain. Your narrative matters in all of the spaces that span from depths of grief to expanse of joy.

Your safety, dignity, and value are of utmost concern. When people are hurt, it does not always mean the person who inflicted the pain will need to be in the healing process. Sometimes there are places of trauma or underdeveloped interpersonal skills that could hinder a person's ability, capacity, or willingness to enter into the process of restoration in relationship.

Mental, emotional, spiritual, physical, and psychological health are important to the interplay of loving relationships. Holistic development needs compassionate care of oneself by other caring individuals. Seeking professional guidance through therapy, counseling, or medical advice along with spiritual direction and meditative practices are important elements to the healing process. Healthy people can influence establishing and reciprocating whole person relationships.

The path toward restoration will be something that involves attention, energy, and intention to seek transformation in individual lives and communities. A commitment to holistic, restorative healing requires time, stamina, and energy. This is a choice made individually that will collectively influence all external relationships. Sometimes people decide to engage in this ongoing development, other times the willingness to engage is not present. This will hinder the work of communal healing.

Healing, though, when it does happen can involve forgiveness. Acknowledging that hurt has happened by one or multiple individuals can lead to the necessary conversations to rebuild relationship. This is a process that can flow from within us as we acknowledge our need to forgive and receive forgiveness. This takes time, energy, and effort. Rebuilding what has been broken is the essence of the arc of creation: what once was intact experienced a severing, division was created, and the process of redemption occurred by showing up again and again.

The space for gathering to break bread on a consistent basis has been present since the beginning and has not stopped being a daily need. Celebration, humility, forgiveness, redemption, and remembrance are all a part of the oxygen of our being. We are showing up at the tables set since Genesis 1 and continuing to daily show up to our need to come together as we look toward the promise of Revelation 22 with a final, amen.

Throughout the stories in Scripture, in whatever is encountered within relationship from goodness to chaos, God has been present and can be found. This concept far exceeds my understanding of how relational redemption can transcend in ways that heal, yet I will continue to sit with these words of restoration by Isaiah in 55:6–12:

> Seek the Lord while he may be found, call upon him while he is near; let the wicked forsake their way, and the unrighteous their thoughts; let them return to the Lord, that he may have mercy on them, and to our God, for he will abundantly pardon. For my thoughts are not your thoughts, nor are your ways my ways, says the Lord. For as the heavens are higher than the earth, so are my ways higher than your ways and my thoughts than your thoughts. For as the rain and the snow come down from heaven, and do not return there until they have watered the earth, making it bring forth and sprout, giving seed to the sower and bread to the eater, so shall my word be that goes out from my mouth; it shall not return to me empty, but it shall accomplish that which I purpose, and succeed in the thing for which I sent it. For you shall go out in joy, and be led back in peace; the mountains and the hills before you shall burst into song, and all the trees of the field shall clap their hands.

At times this process of restoration takes place over many months or years. I have had friends where a chasm in communication has been present. Or times when taking a few steps back offered a better vantage point to seeing a difference of opinion from the other person's viewpoint. There are other people where there is still fog in our way of seeing the way forward. Yet I have not lost hope that one day there could be renewal in relationship. May the unifying presence of God come in these places. I have held near to these words by author and poet Pádraig Ó Tuama as it pertains to the sitting that is needed while awaiting resolve among the people of Northern Ireland.

> Neither I nor the poets I love found the keys to the kingdom of prayer and we cannot force God to stumble over us where we sit. But I know that it's a good idea to sit anyway. So every morning I sit, I kneel, waiting, making friends with the habit of listening, hoping that I'm being listened to. There, I greet God in my own disorder. I say

hello to my chaos, my unmade decisions, my unmade bed, my desire and my trouble. I say hello to distraction and privilege, I greet the day and I greet my beloved and bewildering Jesus. I recognize and greet my burdens, my luck, my controlled and uncontrollable story. I greet my untold stories, my unfolding story, my unloved body, my own love, my own body. I greet the things I think will happen and I say hello to everything I do not know about the day. I greet my own small world and I hope that I can meet the bigger world that day. I greet my story and hope that I can forget my story during the day, and hope that I can hear some stories, and greet some surprising stories during the long day ahead. I greet God, and I greet the God who is more God than the God I greet.

Hello to you all, I say, as the sun rises above the chimneys of North Belfast.

Hello.[3]

The God we greet, and the God bigger than the God we greet, is a Healer. We have all been hurt in relationship and we will heal in relationship. I will live my life believing that redemption can transcend around the table when people linger long, uphold one another with love, listen to bring healing to the pain, offer compassionate care, and speak joyful hope that the best is yet to come.

Elements of Communication

The narrative of Scripture begins with communication and is present throughout the entire movement of the narrative. The notion of interpersonal communication has been on the minds of people for a very long time.[4] People have been talking about food and connection with those around them for centuries. Cooking together over conversation as well as eating together is a way to expand one's relational connection.[5] According to the Mennonite

---

3. Tuama, *In the Shelter*, 244–45.

4. Wood, *Interpersonal Communication*, 2–5.

5. Pollan, *Cooked*, 1–5.

faith tradition, spending time together in sharing stories develops richness to their connectedness.[6]

The opportunity to break bread with others, as well as to have participation in the hospitable space, is not complete without the sharing, through communication, with other human beings for the purpose of connection. Throughout Scripture, meals shared highlighted people gathering and it was a way to acknowledge the Divine as the provider. Throughout the narrative text of Scripture, to share a meal was to share a social interchange.

There were also opportunities around a table to sit with someone when there was disagreement or perceived conflict as well as judgements made around who was with whom around the table. In Psalm 23, a table was set as the place where one would find their enemy. A meal eaten together could be a place for reconciliation to happen. When Jesus ate with the tax collectors in the Gospels it was of high concern for the Pharisees, because he was having a social interaction with people who others in the culture would exclude from their tables.

Around the table was where the Last Supper was shared, Jesus sat with Judas, the man who would use words to betray him within hours. Jesus communicated the love he had for his disciples at this meal, as well as the process of remembering his life after he was no longer with them. This remembrance would be done through communication around the table, through the Eucharist.

Since then, this has been a way that Jesus followers remembered, thanked, and celebrated the life-giving freedom through their Redeemer. As Simone Weil, a mystic, has so clearly written, "At the center of the Catholic religion a little formless matter is found, a little piece of bread."[7] Through the breaking of the bread, Henri Nouwen has written, "A truly Eucharistic life means always sayings thanks to God, always praising God, and always being more surprised by the abundance of God's goodness and love."[8] As Jesus followers remember his abundance through more than

6. Redekop, *Mennonite Society*, 130–41.

7. Weil, *Waiting for God*, 199.

8. Nouwen, *Show Me the Way*, 15.

the nourishment of the bread, words of communication are vital. As we read in Matthew 4:4, "But he answered, 'It is written, "One does not live by bread alone, but by every word that comes from the mouth of God."

Each day there are opportunities to engage in sharing meals together around the table for physical and relational nourishment. Meals can remind people of their dependence on something greater.[9] Leonard Sweet shares, "For Christians, every day is a reminder of the resurrection. Each and every day holds celebratory moments. To live life with eyes wide open will illuminate the resurrection hope just waiting to be celebrated."[10] This is poignant to the way of following Jesus through daily nourishment.

A significant hindrance to following Jesus in an age of significant media obligations and temptations is a screen. According to Dustin Willis, "One of the most countercultural things we can do is have an entire conversation with someone without checking our phone."[11] The screen inhibits communication with the people who are in front of you sharing a meal together. Humanity has the opportunity to set down distraction and engage one another at the table with communication of caring commitment to be inclusive, present, and see this space as one that can offer incarnational care.

The Spirit of understanding, embodying respectful differentiation, having eyes to see, contributing in truth-telling conversations, offering listening ears, utilizing forgiving words, and practicing celebration are seven areas that are important aspects of communication.

Spirit of Understanding

The Triune God exemplifies equality in relationship with the others in the trinity through its oneness, yet its individuality. God, Jesus, and the Holy Spirit are separate, yet make up this unity.

9. Chester, *Meal with Jesus*, 122.

10. Sweet, *Bad Habits of Jesus*, 87.

11. Willis and Clements, *Simplest Way to Change the World*, 59–60.

This portrayal of relationship is the image human beings can embody. People can be differentiated, yet still experience relationship by coming together as a way to love and offer inclusive fellowship. In 2 Corinthians 13:13 Paul's words offer a portrait of this interconnected relationship: "The grace of the Lord Jesus Christ, the love of God, and the communion of the Holy Spirit be with all of you."

The Spirit offers an ability to experience togetherness through transcending communication. Isaiah 11:2 calls this the Spirit understanding. In John 14, Jesus is preparing his disciples for what is to come after the resurrection and he does so by saying the Holy Spirit will come to interpret, counsel, and advocate for humanity. It is through the practice of the Eucharist that the actualization of the Triune God will be experienced within community and we will be able to understand.[12]

The intention of life is not to be experienced alone, although some may try. From isolation to codependency, both ends of the spectrum are causes for ruin in relationships. Differentiated separateness is what builds strong relationships.[13] When people enter into communication to have a shared experience of understanding it is difficult to destroy that relationship.[14]

The space around a table breaking bread together along with communication can be a space that daily can be a way to offer a centering direction in the midst of an ever-changing world. Life changes happen on a consistent basis. It is inescapable as a human. People have been gathering around bread and wine for years, a common experience for humanity. Yet, Milton Brasher-Cunningham, a curator of experiences through music and food writes, "We eat the same meal at Communion each time and yet it is not exactly the same because some have gone and others have joined the circle. We bring new joys and sorrows along with new understandings of how we live with our losses. We have new questions,

---

12. Zizioulas, *Being as Communion*, 81.

13. Perel, *Mating in Captivity*, 25.

14. James, *Assholes*, 140–53.

new hopes, new hungers even as we yearn for new perspectives on things that continue to eat at us."[15]

The unchanging nature of the Holy Spirit will be present to offer understanding at each table where bread is broken together among people. In ordinary days eating granola and sipping on a coffee can emulate breaking bread at an altar, the ever-present sense of the Spirit offers understanding among people to translate, counsel, advocate, or offer wisdom.

Embody Respectful Differentiation

In the intricacies of the creation story according to the Genesis poem, the account of humanity utilizes words of formation with breath, ribs, sleep, bones, and flesh. These are words that are spoken embodiment, not just an idea of bodies, but actual living and breathing bodies. Genesis 2:7 explains, "Then the Lord God formed man from the dust of the ground and breathed into his nostrils the breath of life; and the man became a living being." The text continues with the words of the formation of Adam's partner, Eve, in Genesis 2:21–23, "So the Lord God caused a deep sleep to fall upon the man, and he slept; then he took one of his ribs and closed up its place with flesh. And the rib that the Lord God has taken from the man he made into a woman and brought her to the man. Then the man said, 'this is bone of my bones, and flesh of my flesh.'" Humanity is embodied in the flesh of bodies, empowered by internal functions that allow us to think, feel, reason, and engage with others.

Each human is an image bearer of the *Imago Dei*. There are at times similarities; yet there are stark differences on an internal and external basis in personalities, preferences, and experiences. Respect for one another is of the utmost importance. The collective nature of humanity creates a montage of beings inhabiting planet earth. Representation of flesh and blood are humans fashioned in

15. Brasher-Cunningham, *Keeping the Feast*, 53.

the image of the loving Trinitarian belonging of God, Jesus, and Holy Spirit.

As a part of the trinity, Jesus became fully human, yet was fully divine. John 1:14 says, "And the Word became flesh and lived among us, and we have seen his glory, the glory as of a father's only son, full of grace and truth." Jesus also prepared the way for the distinction of the Holy Spirit to be present on earth, by saying these words in John 14:25–26 "I (Jesus) have said these things to you while I am still with you. But the Advocate, the Holy Spirit, whom the Father will send in my name will teach you everything and remind you of all that I have said to you." The communication is experienced on a number of levels within the functionality of the Trinity.

God breathed life into Adam and Eve. Jesus came to life by breathing the air of earth. The Holy Spirit is referred to as the wind that blows where it pleases in John 3:8. The flow of breath and wind give imagery to the masterful creation of living within the embodied mystery of our skin. Trauma therapist Resmaa Menakem articulates masterfully these words regarding our body: "The body, not the thinking brain, is where we experience most of our pain, pleasure, and joy, and where we process most of what happens to us. It is also where we do most of our healing, including our emotional and psychological healing. And it is where we experience resilience and a sense of flow."[16] Our bodies are intended for pleasure; although painful trauma has permeated each life, we have the opportunity to experience proximity gathering at tables with other bodies as a way to heal, grow in trust, and experience delight. Our bodies need physical and relational nourishment on a daily basis.

Addressing our pain and trauma in proximity to others can offer opportunities to heal in the presence of one another. This is a process of building trust and asking permission which is vitally important in communication. A part of this experience takes place through respecting each person's physical space. For instance, some people greet people with a hand shake, hug, or kiss on the cheek. It is important to ask permission before you attempt to engage someone physically. If you pray a blessing before a meal, ask

16. Menakem, *My Grandmother's Hands*, 12.

for consent to hold the hand of another next to you before you reach out for it. Physical touch may not be natural, preferred, or desired by the people with which you share a meal; which is why it is important to honor proximity with consensual permission when touch is involved.

Bodies have been violated, dishonored, abused, and taken advantage of throughout history. Respectfully honoring another person and their preferences for touch will offer profound honor. Each person, every time, deserves the opportunity to decide if they want to engage in touch. Kindly ask and respect the answer.

Differentiation of physical space can help to build communication that is mutually agreed upon through equity and equality. This reflects the Divine Trinitarian relationship, distinct to the others, yet mysteriously connected to create belonging.

The altar is a table that is created to remember, offer thanksgiving, and celebrate in a way that invites our physical presence. Being with another person in physical proximity is a privilege that is at times susceptible to feeling exposed.

Honoring each other's experience can help to foster environments where transformational healing can take place. Throughout years of research on the body, Dr. Bessel A. Van der Kolk has noted, "People can learn to control and change their behavior, but only if they feel safe enough to experiment with new solutions. The body keeps the score: If trauma is encoded in heartbreaking and gut-wrenching sensations, then our first priority is to help people move out of fight-or-flight states, organize their perception of danger, and manage relationships."[17] In order to feel safe in an environment, a person's differentiated space needs to be respected. Therefore trust can be built through using embodied communication.

To live embodied is to experience the present moment in the body.[18] Embodied work allows for verbal and nonverbal communication to be expressed in a way that allows for all of the senses of the body to be awake and alert. The ordinary moments can then

17. Van der Kolk, *Body Keeps the Score*, 351.

18. Van der Kolk, *Body Keeps the Score*, 223.

transcend the breaking of bread to experience internal transformational kneading of our longing for meaning.

Eyes to See

All throughout the New Testament stories of blindness are connected to miracles—people who physically cannot see, born blind or over the course of their lives became blind.

In our culture today, how often do people who do not have physical blindness choose to live with their eyes shut in order to avoid pain? Or how often does one's inability to see clearly lead to racism, exclusion, judgment, intolerance, or hurt? Is this because the idea of changing a perspective would require too much internal work? Or highlight places where expansion of understanding on a topic is needed? What if open eyes would allow for a broader understanding of another person? What if living with eyes wide open led to apologizing for pain inflicted upon another person?

Actively living in communal relationship can help to shed light on reality, yet how often are people avoiding relationship as a way not to deal with conflict? It is a brave choice to ask someone for help to see perceived blind spots in actions, behaviors, and responses. It is another thing to do the resilient work that is related to, yet not limited to, the therapeutic process needed to bring the chaos, trauma, or pain into sight.

When people try on clothing the next step after the outfit is in place is to go stand in front of a mirror and stare at yourself. Yet a mirror does not always accurately portray the fullness of what is present based on lighting and angles of the setup of the reflective glass. Yet, rarely do people leave the house without the stamp of approval from a piece of glass.

Why do people communicate with the external world with so much more attention than the internal? Tweezers, razors, nail clippers, lip gloss, makeup, hair product, lotions, hair dryers, curling irons, straighteners, shaving cream, essential oils, moisturizing skin cream, and on and on it goes with the list of products that are used frequently to tend to what other people see. Granted, these forms of self-care are helpful to our desired external look, yet our internal appearance will manifest itself in the external.

What are the things that are a part of caring for the internal? Whole person development sounds like a well-balanced idea, yet needs internal communication and care. Strength in developing our verbal skills and emotional intelligence is vital to communication. Relationships that have these skills are strong, and have held up through the test of time.

When people attempt to "save face," it implies that they are working to manage their own image and forsake seeing another person with their eyes wide open. If people are willing to see the muck and the mire that are present, then there is an honesty and transparency that allows for what is really happening to be seen. My friend, Arlita, who embodies inspiration and wisdom, asks people of importance in her life on a regular basis questions that invite other people's perspective of how they experience her words and actions. These questions will bring to light quite quickly the impact of actions. Our intentions might not always be received with the same impact we hope, which is why communication is helpful to clear the air of misunderstanding. If something is unclear, ask curious questions.

Communication of our weakness, brokenness, and pain are a part of each personal narrative and therefore each relationship. It is a part of being a human. Mutually working together in relationship to experience holiness will illuminate the experience of the trinity's equity with one another. Yet, to see without splintered eyesight, relationships can be strengthened through apologies, forgiveness, and reconciliation.

Restoration of sight is a miracle for humility. Mark 10:51–52 says, "Then Jesus said to him, 'What do you want me to do for you?' The blind man said to him, 'My teacher, let me see again.' Jesus said to him, 'Go your faith has made you well. Immediately he regained his sight and followed him the way.'" May the trinity guide people, with open eyes, into telling the truth to oneself and others as way of care.

Open eyes also will create opportunities to see bravery, beauty, joy, kindness, and compassion. Seeing clearly will allow for the eyes of the heart to be opened to healing, love, and acceptance. Open eyes will see the Light.

Contribute in Truth-Telling Conversations

When something painful happens with another person, the flight, fight, flee, or freeze methods of handling the conflict come as quick as ants do to a fruit rollup on a hot day. There is nothing in my self-protective flesh that wants to offer any level of my openness to another person if I been hurt. Or if there has been conflict, you had better believe the idea of "forgive and forget" that some people preach is an expired concept.

When I am hurt, I want to be heard. I want to be seen. I want my pain to matter. I want to be understood. I want someone to say "I value you, and I am sorry I hurt you." I want someone to listen and acknowledge that my pain matters. Even if the hurt or pain is not fully understood by another person, I find it loving to have someone be present in working towards healing from that pain.

This is the human desire because we are created in the flow of a community that respected one another with mutuality.

As an adult I have grown to appreciate these words that represent essential building blocks in a strong community:

Reconciliation.

Truth-telling.

Care.

Forgiveness.

Encouragement.

Respect.

As a child I was very shy. We would have memorization contests in elementary school and then be chosen to recite our poems at local and state competitions. I remember being terrified of being in front of others: What if I forget what I was supposed to say? What will people think of me? What if I mess up?

Lo and behold each year I was chosen. And each year I would want to hide away from being in front of others. As I continued through elementary school my parents enrolled me in classes at the local civic theater. I was terrified to be in front of people. Over time, this experience propelled me to the stage, at front and center of an audience. I found it was easier to act like someone else, rather than be myself.

As I entered high school, I found my voice to share my thoughts and opinions. This was helpful in learning more and more of what it meant to be myself. But then there was that one day in particular in freshman English class when a fellow classmate made a derogatory comment about the way my body looked. I can still remember the sting of his words as I tried to hold in the embarrassment that was coming over me until the bell rang for the next class.

It was such a vulnerable time in my formation of understanding who I was and who I wanted to become. It was throughout these years of being afraid to use my own voice when I learned the value of truth-telling as a way to advocate for myself and others, of speaking words of life to other people and standing up for those who are being marginalized. It was through this time that I was able to conceptualize what it would mean in the future to stand up for other people. Speaking words of compassionate advocacy can be a healing balm.

Daily there are opportunities to voice words of life or death to other people. Though it requires deep care for oneself and others to share honestly, it is necessary to speak up. Walk with kind conviction in the office. Write a letter. Ask to speak with the person who is speaking hurtful words. Put energy into the hard work of navigating to cultivate true peace, with nothing artificial added.

Words can grow the fruits of the Spirit and produce a harvest of plenty. Sure, it can take a lot of time to cultivate, but daily careful intentionality will create places of peace. Some of the memories I have as it pertains to speaking Truth are some of the hardest, funniest, and most awkward conversations I have had with other people. These conversations have happened when I have lived with people and idiosyncrasies are highlighted. There are times a microscope has been needed to to examine painful experiences and carefully dissect what was taking place. Another time it was going to buy ice cream together at midnight was a way to share a peace offering after an argument. And there have been a fair share of conversations that have started, "can you help me understand . . . ?" As we seek to experience Truth, communication is needed.

When understanding has happened with mutuality these have been some of the most rewarding experiences. Speaking Truth is necessary and creates spaces for understanding each other. The air is cleared, understanding can be reached, and at times when differences persist there can still be respect.

Caring for other people with words involves understanding the embodiment of communicating truthfully. This is a practice of speaking and listening as another person shares their thoughts and feelings. This is the dialect of love, to communicate value to my neighbor by truth-telling with a compassionate disposition. At times, it is to understand and engage in acknowledging the conflict that is present.

Truth-telling can unearth conflicted ideas which can be the precursor of healthy, fruitful, and caring relationships. Conversations built upon love can be painful, yet also healing. When there is care in communication the light shining between people can produce an effervescent energy in the exchange of words. Often conflicted communication is avoided by people who do not want to engage in their own pain of being hurt or recognize that the other person could be holding pain. This can entail a process of having a difficult conversation. Some people prefer only to see the positive and avoid engaging in the struggle at all cost. This can lead to stunted development or can suffocate the relationship if the conflict is not aired.

When there are disagreements, the primary hope is to uphold respect for understanding each other along with holding space to work through the disagreement. There can be risk involved in hoping for understanding, but conversations can produce clarity. Curious questions can offer insight and understanding. This space can help to eliminate the unsettledness that is being experienced.

It is important in communication to uphold fruit-bearing values that offer each person dignity, respect, and love. This pertains to difficult and conflicted conversations as well. Taking time to have the conversation with these things present, communicates care. Speaking directly with another person where there is mutuality will enhance a relationship. In order to have a robust interchange, people speaking the Truth in love will result in each person experiencing respect.[19]

When people speak directly with one another, rather than behind their back, it will help to clear the air when conflict is present. All too often people avoid having conflicted conversations because of self-preservation, pride, avoidance, or uncertainty of how to have the conversation. If a relationship no longer shares the same values it will be hard for truth-telling to be shared or received in a way that can move through the disagreement to a fruit-bearing relationship.

Conflict is a part of what takes place on a regular basis. It is inevitable that there will be grievances from the day that could infiltrate into the time around the table. This can become part of the fabric of the learning within relationships, as well as sharing in transparency, what is taking place. People must recognize that conflict is a part of relationships that has the potential to enhance growth and intimacy.

Often the role of the one who keeps the peace is something that is glorified in relationships, yet too many times this is a false sense of peace. Sweeping the disagreements under the rugs throughout a house is a lazy way to handle conflict. Courage is needed to show up in a conversation with one's full self in order to be transparent in the misunderstanding. Speaking with direct kindness offers the hope in mending the relationship to set people up to thrive.[20]

Thriving communication needs to have consent from everyone involved. If people do not want to show up in the conversation, it will suffer. If people do not want to sacrifice to make changes in telling the truth or receiving the truth in the relationship; it could

19. Diamant and Cooper, *Living a Jewish Life*, 149.
20. Scazzero, *Emotionally Healthy Spirituality*, 32–34.

be coming to a point of taking a break or it could have come to an end. Bearing witness to one another's experience will create a deeper bond of understanding. Dr. Christine Pohl has written, "We are not called to create ideal families, communities, or congregations. Building faithful communities of truth and hospitality, however, is at the heart of our grateful response to the one who 'became flesh and lived among us . . . full of grace and truth.'"[21]

God walked with Adam and Eve in the garden of Eden. After they ate of the fruit they realized they were exposed and went to hide, God went looking for them. The Creator God intentionally went towards their shame-filled hiding and asked, "Where are you?" This question came out of loving care with a desire to restore relationship.

How kind, to start the conversation with "Where are you?" These three words offer loving inquiry.

Offer Listening Ears

"This morning, I was sitting in my chair, listening." This sentence was said more times than I can count by one of my dearest, most discerning, and sassiest of friends, Jackie. Her life was one of listening. A social worker by trade, she was a woman who cared deeply for people through her hospitable care of people's physical nourishment at her table, where she also cared for their souls. The veil of heaven was near to this woman as she embodied a closeness with God through the years of cultivating a relationship of listening. There were seasons when she asked me questions about things I have not ever uttered words about. Or the times she looked at me and said, "Take it or leave it, but I wonder . . ." and then she would fill in the rest of the sentence with words directly correlating to something that she has heard from her time alone in silence.

The time Jackie spent alone with the Triune God of wisdom allowed her to have words of nourishment to share in abundance. She did this by setting her table with detail, thoughtfulness, and

---

21. Pohl, *Living Into Community*, 176.

whimsy that made you want to stay. Yet when the meal was over at her house she did not let you help clean up, because she said it gave her time to recount the meal while she washed the dishes to listened to anything left unsaid. She was connected to the Trinity's voice, because she had spent hours daily listening to know the voice of the eternal.

"The first duty of love is to listen," says philosopher Paul Tillich. Those who are present at the table can participate in communication, but they can also listen for those who have not shared and then welcome each voice to use their words to take part in the conversation. They are listening to spoken words as well as what has not been verbally shared. When words are communicated it can be used as a way to enhance a person's understanding with a more prolific vocabulary because it is being modeled through conversation. The art of listening around the table begins with people simply asking for the things that they desire, which in turn encourages people to make eye contact, which opens up opportunity to form relationship.

Grand Rapids has an adorable shop named Sweetie-licious Bakery with award-winning pies where I was able to work while living in beautiful west Michigan. The regular twelve-to-twelve shift consisted of everything from making stock pots full of pie filling to starting cookie dough (inevitably Trisha would finish, every single time) to cracking dozens of eggs for the fluffiest quiches, to learning the art of zesting and making dark chocolate ganache; and there were consistently a number of customers who would approach the bakery case looking for that sweet treat for that perfect occasion.

As we were working one day I overheard a conversation from the front counter while I was mixing crumble-pie topping, I could hear a kind man's voice asking one of the employees which pie was her favorite. They shared back and forth about their favorite sweet treats. As they continued to exchange words in their dialogue it was clear that the tempo of the conversation was no longer gleeful about raspberry pie and the smooth textures of cream pies; this elderly man appeared to have a little bit of a shaky tone. I remember noticing how the conversation unfolded as the question was posed so sincerely by my coworker, "Is this pie you are buying for something special?" The man, with tears in his eyes said, "Yes, it would be my anniversary this week, fifty years." Then, wiping the tears from his eyes with the white cloth handkerchief from his back pocket, he continued, "But my wife has passed just six months ago. So I will enjoy this piece of pie and think of her." She looked into his eyes and said, "I am so sorry for your loss. This piece is on me. I hope you have a beautiful time remembering her life." He gratefully received this piece of pie, picked up his cane, and walked away. She stood and watched him walk out the door, offering honor to their conversation. She then took money out of her purse from under the counter and paid for his pie, as she then wiped a tear from her eye.

It is listening for the words spoken and it is staying in the evolution of the conversation to see what words have yet to be shared or spoken into existence. Her presence offered dignity over a conversation separated by a pink countertop with a piece of pie. Although strangers, she let the reality of his story affect her response and responded with such empathy.

Conversations have tones, spoken and unspoken. Intentions and impacts. Direct and indirect. Whatever the topic of conversation, there is something that is intended and something that is behind the words that come out of someone's mouth.

Will we be people who listen to the conversations in our own heads before we speak them to see if what we are about to say is what we would like to communicate? Will we be people who listen kindly, because often behind what is spoken is something deeper, a longing, desire, or hope that is being communicated?

In an interview Krista Tippett had with David Isay, founder of an organization called StoryCorps, which focuses on persevering stories, she shares, "We're listening creatures. That listening is an everyday art, and it's a social technology."[22] To elicit understanding, one must listen.

---

22. Tippett, "Listening as an Act of Love," 43:57–44:10.

Utilize Forgiving Words

A few years ago, I had dinner with my friend, Katie, who I had met in 2004. We literally became friends within minutes of meeting each other, one of those instantaneous connections. After years of friendship and quite a few changes in our stories we were having dinner as a way to catch up after a number of moves, relationships, hurtful losses, and new loves. Yet at this particular dinner I had a posture of arrogance and judgement towards decisions that she was making in her life as it pertained to faith.

I look back and recognize how pathetically unkind I was as I pretended to listen, yet silently judged her choices. There was nothing about that night that I look back on and feel proud of as I had let differences be a source of severing in my care of listening to her share.

A few more years had passed with limited conversation on my part. I was skeptical of her life choices and instead of trying to understand I created judgmental distance. One day in my time of meditative silence, I was deeply saddened by the hurt I had ensued. I began writing her an apology letter after I was so saddened by how I had treated her with my arrogant judgement.

After finishing up the letter, I could not find her current address or her phone when I attempted to text her, which led me to send her a message on social media. But I received no response. For all I knew, she did not want to have communication, which I could not blame her for on any level. My words and internal actions were cruel.

Time passed as the letter sat next to my bed, under a pile of books. As I was preparing to move I was stacking the books in a wooden crate and as I picked up the dusty letter and thought, "Here is to hoping that maybe one day I can apologize," and tucked it inside of a book to pack.

One day, out of the blue, I received a message from an unknown number with the words, "Hello, Julia. It is Katie. I am just seeing your message from social media, when can we connect?"

My heart dropped.

Then I mustered up the wherewithal to ask her for her address to send her a letter that was written years ago.

She gave it to me.

The following day I mailed the letter.

A few days after receiving the letter, she called me.

My heart sank deeper. I had no idea what the conversation would hold. All I wanted to do was send the letter and move on. I was embarrassed by what I had done years earlier and the ways I had hurt her by my judgment.

We set up a time to call and without missing a beat, she cheerfully said, "Julia, I have missed you."

Tears welled up in my eyes and I responded, "I have missed you too."

I continued to own the pain that I had caused. I apologized by naming my judgment and arrogance. I apologized, as I had stepped away rather than entering into what I did not understand.

She assured me that all was forgiven.

Sporadic communication took place in the upcoming years due to distance. She invited me to her house while I was on a recent vacation near her home; as I sat in the Uber on my way to her home I was silently anticipating what it would be like to be face to face after a number of years had gone by since we had been together. I was nervous as I stood at her front door and knocked. Yet she flung opened the door, joyfully squealed, and went to hug me, while saying, "Julia, it's been too long!"

To which I responded, "I am so sorry."

She said, "Oh girl, that is the past and we have talked through all that. We have now, we can start here."

I was humbled, as I was a recipient of her kind forgiveness which brought us back together.

To experience an apology or granted forgiveness is to experience reunification in love. In order to forgive or to have forgiveness there is a need to let things go, to release unmet expectations, and to grieve the pain of what has been lost in the process.[23] When people take time to reflect on what has taken place in their lives

---

23. Brown, *Rising Strong*, 150.

and in the lives of those around them, there is a chance to recognize what has kept people from connecting with each other. In Matthew 26:26–28, Jesus recognized the need to come to the table and remember the forgiveness we have experienced. He invited people to take part in communion as a place of remembrance of what he has done in order to offer freedom from the disruptions in relationships. The table is representative of a space open for all to live forgiven and walk away with motivation to love.

A posture of humility can strengthen a relationship by healing the pain that has taken place between people.[24] There is power in communicating through confession, as James 5:16 speaks of: "Confess your sins to one another." There is room to experience freedom with one another when you are working together to commune and come together for the purpose of experiencing freedom from sin and walking in forgiveness together.[25]

Forgiveness requires you to encounter pain as well as the hurt that surrounds that pain.[26] There is a humility that is needed to reflect on the emotion surrounding the pain, in order to forgive. Desmond Tutu shares, "To forgive is not to pretend that what happened did not happen. Healing does not draw a veil over the hurt. Rather, healing and reconciliation demand an honest reckoning. For Jesus followers, Jesus Christ sets the pattern for forgiveness and reconciliation."[27]

In order to love and receive the love that God intended, we must allow forgiveness to take place for healing to occur. As Grandma Rhoda Showalter shares, "Time will heal all wounds, unless they are infected."[28] We must take time to heal through forgiveness for relationships to be reflective and restored. Gordon Smith shares, "The table is never merely about our forgiveness. It is also about the forgiveness we offer to others. The Lord's Supper

24. Hellerman, *When the Church Was a Family*, 152–55.

25. Milne, *We Belong Together*, 82.

26. Milne, *We Belong Together*, 149–56.

27. Tutu and Tutu, *Book of Forgiving*, 23–24.

28. Kristin Green, interviewed by author, Goshen, Indiana, October 19, 2015.

enables us to live the gospel, to embody what it means to be a people who are transformed by the good news."[29]

Time for reflection can offer a place to tell the story of forgiveness at the table. It is through humility and repentance that relationship is restored. The Aramaic definition of repentance is "returning home." Old things have passed away and things have become new, as it is said by Paul in 2 Corinthians 5:17.[30] Tim Chester shares, "Generous hospitality leads to reconciliation. It is expressed forgiveness. Unresolved conflict can't be ignored when we gather around the meal table; you can't eat in silence without realizing there's an issue to address."[31]

When there is conflict, opposing thoughts, or a disagreement among people in a community, it is vitally important to stay present in the necessary conversations that will help to foster movement towards reconciling understanding. There are times, though, when people avoid conflict, will not engage in the conversation, or are abusive in their behaviors which therefore can lead to a parting of ways. Sometimes necessary endings are imperative if people are not offering mutuality in relationship. If respect, consideration, and dignity are no longer a part of the ethos of interactions, truthtelling cannot be received.

Relationships that are mutual, honest, and congruent require energy. As Dietrich Bonhoeffer has said, "The person who loves their dream of community will destroy community, but the person who loves those around them will create community."[32]

Amen and amen.

If we just sit around and dream about the idea of community we will destroy it. How often have you found yourself intrigued with the idea of living among others yet the intrigue quickly turns to skepticism because of the probability of being out of control of the impact of another person's behavior? Or how often have you found yourself wanting to control the actions, words, or impact of

29. Smith, *Holy Meal*, 57–65.

30. Sweet and Viola, *Jesus Speaks*, 8.

31. Chester, *Meal with Jesus*, 48–49.

32. Bonhoeffer, *Life Together*, 27.

another person because you do not want to get hurt? These are realities in relationships, but undealt-with trauma will keep a person from moving into healthy, life-giving interactions. Redemption must take place to move us towards another person to restore life.

The separation that is present within relationship with God and each other will create disruption. Isolated from perfect union is like trying to paddle down a river, but instead steering the canoe back and forth on the banks of the river. The banks represent chaos and rigidity all the while the middle of the river would hold well being.[33] Fractured relationships can leave people in disarray all while Jesus came to earth as the redemptive Healer to offer a life of transformational wholeness and well being.

Practice Celebration

Can you think of a noteworthy event when all seemed to promote joyful celebration in the world? The opportunity to experience celebration is a sacred encounter. Moments that take one's breath away happen often at celebratory events. One birthday it came in the form of a surprise gift of hang-gliding for the afternoon. Another time a trip in a village ended with a celebration of staying in yurts for the night. Expansive charcuterie tables, dinners with lavish foods, and exquisite drinks people are still talking about can all be elements of adding to a celebration. At a recent birthday party I attended a shooting star soared across the moonlit sky. These are definitions of magical, celebratory moments.

Then there are moments when it is time to celebrate when unmet hopes, an incomplete guest list, unforeseen weather, or unprecedented events cloud the intentions of celebrations. Smiles and tears can accent one another quite well, it is an irony to celebratory events. What seem like opposing emotions, joy and sorrow, I have come to believe are needed companions. When we engage the gamut of our whole selves to come celebrate, something within our souls touch eternity. It is a great mystery, yet it is one deeply celebrated.

33. Siegel and Bryson, *Whole-Brain Child*, 12.

Yada is a word used in the Old Testament over 900 times that means, "To know deeply or intimately, to be known." This word refers to intimacy with God and at times others.[34] Humankind was created in the image of connection with the Divine Triune God. Debra Hirsch describes "spirituality, a vast longing that drives us beyond ourselves in an attempt to connect with, to probe and to understand our world. And beyond that, it is the inner compulsion to connect with the Eternal Other, which is God.[35]

In celebratory communities people can magnify what it means to live as their truest selves, as this is a reflection of the *Imago Dei*. Celebration is a wonderful place for connection among desire and a longing to manifest. Culture, society, and the church are places that can cultivate rituals of corporate parties. Bounty was a part of the Genesis poem; the creation story commenced as a celebration of life. The trinity is creative from the spoken words all throughout the Genesis poem. They actively engaged in the details that make up a beautiful story of speaking earth into existence.

Creation has a language that speaks to celebration through the vibrancy of color, texture, sounds of creatures, lighting that changes throughout the day, smells, and sights. It speaks to the full-bodied expression based on what hemisphere you are in during the celebration. The assortment of expression creates a space for any person's preference.

Childhood memories from outdoor camping have influenced my affinity for nature. Growing up, every summer we would go camping with a number of other families. The bike rides, tubing on a river, meals over the fire, and copious amounts of s'mores were among a few of my favorite things. Now, as an adult, I have been thankful for the continued outdoor invitations to camp and linger in conversation around the open fire late into the night.

One of the most memorable birthdays that I have as an adult was when I was living in a house with six other people in North Carolina. This particular year I shared my desire for my January

34. Yada, https://www.blueletterbible.org/lang/lexicon/lexicon.cfm?t=kjv&strongs=h3045

35. Hirsch, *Redeeming Sex*, 26.

birthday celebration, to go camping. My housemates humored me and played along with my ideas, but acknowledging where we lived it was too cold to go camping in January. We agreed that a few of us going to a movie would be a more realistic option.

After the movie, we arrived home, walked up the deck stairs, and upon opening the back door there were sounds of crickets chirping from inside the house. The smell of embers burning in our indoor living room stone fireplace wafted through the house. As I turned toward the fire place, a fort of sheets had been constructed with all of our adult sleeping bags laid out. Camping chairs, flannels, and s'mores were awaiting my "camping" birthday sleepover on this snowy January night. We sat for hours talking, and thanks to technology the crickets sounded all night. It was a moment in my life when all was right in the world, a simple celebration as my desires were heard and the housemates created a celebratory memory I treasure to this day.

Important moments in life offer invitation to pause and acknowledge the joy that is taking place. Jesus' first miracle in revealing himself as the Messiah was turning water into wine. This story has been one of the best-known wedding stories around, because it was more than imagined.

Celebrations that have loving intentionality are the icing on the cake. Gathering people together as a way of honor requires selflessness.

> Ask, and it will be given you; search, and you will find; knock, and the door will be opened for you. For everyone who asks receives, and everyone who searches finds, and for everyone who knocks, the door will be opened. Is there anyone among you who, if your child asks for bread, will give a stone? Or if the child asks for a fish, will give a snake? If you then, who are evil, know how to give good gifts to your children, how much more will your Father in heaven give good things to those who ask him. (Matthew 7:7–11)

The goodness of God offers to us what we desire; it is vulnerable to ask others to do the same.

Each celebration has the opportunity to highlight ordinary things that are enjoyed by the person who is on the receiving end of the party. The array of celebration has included, but not limited to, Haley and Brandon's crafted meals set on placements with coordinating plates, a deck with abundant seating surrounded by individually placed plants, Ashley's gluten-free carrot cake, gathering together around a hand-built table for a toast, cinnamon rolls and coffee for hours, charcuterie boards that take up the entire table, a gift of a bike, parties where all are welcome to bring in the new year, oodles of sparkling water, lingering breakfasts made in a cast iron skillet, a surprise stop at a favorite farm, spoken and written blessings, and the list could go on and on.

There are times, though, when celebrations have also been a complete flop. People are not there, the present that was ordered did not come, the cake was burnt, weather inhibited an outdoor event, or people entirely missed the mark on gift-giving. Things do not always turn out in the exact ways that people would hope. These are the moments when we can choose to acknowledge that we make mistakes and we can apologize for what we took part in as the ball was dropped. Then other times things just are not the way we had hoped and that can be acknowledged too as a loss.

At times, the desire to be seen is unmet and you can feel lonely. There are times when people are excluded, which is so painful. The gathering that was created in Genesis had space for each person; creation was made to function together to be fruitful image bearers of the Divine. There are times, though, when people follow selfishness that can create disruption in the connection in relationship, when the celebrations do not mirror the Trinity's idea of celebratory space for all to come to the table. Whether the people around a table are relatives, friends, or family, there could be fractions among the people. The table can be a leveling space where people can expose pain or embrace intimacy.

Yet, in the most idealistic of times, when the stars of communication align or the most isolating times of exclusion, the Triune God sees each person in the darkness of silent nights; or when the dawn of day is perfectly shining, the Divine has a place for each person at the table.

There are necessary preparations that help create an environment where guests enjoy a delicious meal for the sake of celebration. However, there are also things that can be done to prepare to make guests feel welcome to come as they are. Jesus delights in those who host because it mirrors what he has done as he breaks bread and pours out wine.[36] In the Mennonite culture, J. Craig Haas shares his thoughts on the value of participation in festivities by stating, "Participation in the festive reenactments of that story brings us closer to our own cultural and historical roots . . . BUT people must participate."[37] Celebrations can be a time for people to be known through engaging in the sacred privilege of intimate relationship. Honoring friends, family, and even enemies illuminates the story of Scripture that all are welcomed with a seat at the table.

Celebrate intentionally.

Celebrate well.

Celebrate often.

Reflection Questions

1. In what ways does your communication speak fruitfulness through love, joy, peace, patience, kindness, goodness, faithfulness, gentleness, and self-control? In what ways can you expand your capacity to communicate care through your actions and words?

2. How can you foster an environment conducive to inclusion, growth, and intimacy around your table, even if it includes conflict, tension, or differences?

3. Who is present at your table in need of forgiveness? From whom might you need to seek forgiveness? With whom do

---

36. Webster, *Table Grace*, 21–22.

37. Haas, *Readings from Mennonite Writings*, 304.

you need to humbly seek reconciliation, who may not be present at the table?

4. In what ways do you celebrate around your table? Are there any ways that you would like this to expand?

Part Seven

Conclusion, Yes and Amen

Woody Allen once said that 80 percent of success is simply showing up . . . "showing up" means facing into your thoughts, emotions, and behaviors willingly, with curiosity and kindness.[1]

SUSAN DAVID

May the Lord bless his people with peace!

PSALM 29:11B

Amen. Come, Lord Jesus! The grace of the Lord Jesus be with all of the saints. Amen.

REVELATION 22:20B–21

So BE IT, AMEN. When it is time for a story to end, what are the thoughts that come to mind? What emotions are ready to erupt when the last line is read? Do you spend time imagining how the story might end? What do you do once the story has come to the point of closure?

1. David, *Emotional Agility*, 11.

The end is often connected with the word "forever," or the word "eternity." I was seven when my grandma died and this was my first encounter with the idea of finality and death and forever. I remember asking a question about this word, "eternity," that I did not understand. My mom said, "Eternity is hard to understand, but the longing for it is already within us."

As I laid in bed that night, I remember shoving my face into my pillow trying to comprehend eternity. I said into my pillow with a muffled voice, "Eternity. Eternity. Eternity. What would our bodies do for eternity?" Weeks turned into months and then months into years that I would fall asleep thinking about this word: eternity.

Years upon years would go by and I would still be asking questions. They were not all connected to eternity. They were, though, existential in nature.

Asking questions.

Pondering.

Waking up with questions.

Falling asleep asking questions.

I cannot remember my life without asking questions.

The questions have been innocent at times. Un-manicured. Unedited. Raw, yet full of wonder.

And somehow night after night, year after year, I believed someone was listening to these questions. And at some point each night I would fall asleep still speaking my questions out loud.

There is something about asking questions that transcend the ordinary moments to connect with another. These remind me of those questions about the meaning of all of this and what eternity has to do with it—the unification with the Trinity, the connected nature of all becoming well.

One day when all has become well, there will be a table that will have white linens, as Revelation 19 has recorded from the vision the author John received. This will be a table for celebration of the eternal union of community with the Triune God.

I find it hard to understand, but the longing for eternity is already within the fragility of our lives. Over the past three years

I have had two very close friends receive these words: "You have a terminal illness." There is nothing quite like sitting with people who are aware of the impending finality of life here on earth. As I talked with Kim on a number of occasions over tea during her two-year stint with terminal cancer before she met eternity in the spring, she would say, "The only thing I know to do is to show up to each day, unless a miracle extends my life, I will meet my end sooner than I imagined."

Just a few weeks after Kim met eternity, I sat at a table with two beloved friends, Jackie shared with Cindy and me that she had just received a terminal diagnosis. We were brokenhearted, as we sat at the Jackie's table, with tears in our eyes at the thought of the looming days ahead.

Over the years we have shared space together around so many tables in a number of environments, yet on this day we found ourselves eating strawberry shortcake sprinkled with our tears and questions of what it means to walk towards the veil of life on earth before she met the eternal God in early fall.

Sitting in stillness in grief is to sit *shiva* as is practiced in the Jewish culture. To stay with someone while there are unknown questions or pain in the midst of loss is to offer a loving presence. It is a unifying, vulnerable, and an invitational opportunity to participate with another person communicating care with presence rather than words.

Here on earth, in between what is now and what is to come still holds questions that at times are terrifying, sad, funny, nuanced, raw, innocent, hopeful, curious, and some painful to mutter. There are times that it seems more enticing to settle for avoidance rather than sitting with unanswered questions. I do, though, believe that there is someone listening.

This seems similar to the approach of the table by quickly eating a meal with the attempts to silencing the lingering, unresolved questions present. Eating alone, together, can attempt to numb the disconnect present in relational intimacy.

Connection has been the essence of meaningful belonging from the beginning. The Divine trinity is present, ready to transcend the space around the table. For now, a number of tables are before us here in community, may we forfeit lives of isolation and choose to live embodied with grace amidst the perceived chaos with one another.

May we be fruitful people. May we have the grace to be fruitful even among all that is chaotic and out of control on earth.

May we be people of peace as we live on earth.

The table is a gathering place, a place of invitation where people come and sit, participate in the shared meal, as well as communicate while sharing this space. The *ecclesia* modeled this practice as a way to engage in the relational interactions that mirror the Triune God. The building of this table is kneaded by present people.

Creator God, Jesus, and the Holy Spirit are love. Spending time around the table creates an opportunity to extend that kindness of love. Romans 12:9–13 offers encouragement to love well: "Let love be genuine; hate what is evil, hold fast to what is good; love one another with mutual affection; outdo one another in showing honor. Do not lag in zeal, be ardent in spirit, and serve the Lord. Rejoice in hope, be patient in suffering, persevere in prayer. Contribute to the needs of the saints; extend hospitality to strangers."

Leonard Sweet shares this idea in his book *Tablet to Table*: "Narraphors are stories made with metaphors that help us understand world, God, and ourselves in a clearer way. Narraphors are the *lingua franca* of the Christian faith. They are table talk."[2] The table must be a place of invitation for the stories of the Bible to become metaphors for how we live our lives. The space around a table is an opportunity to have sacred encounters with other people with the purpose of bringing the hopeful narrative of Scripture to life here on earth. This is the foretelling of a great banquet of heaven that is written about in Revelation 19. The distance that has been present between earth and the eternal oneness with the Triune God will be no more. The finality of the longing will be over and there will be a seat at the table of eternity with abundant

---

2. Sweet, *From Tablet to Table*, 3–4.

acceptance, love, and belonging. Hafiz, a poet, offers this insight in his poem "Tired of Speaking Sweetly":

> Love wants to reach out . . . break all our teacup talk of
> God . . .
> Ripping from your grip all all those toys in the world
> That bring you no joy.
> Love sometimes gets tired of speaking sweetly . . .
> The Beloved sometimes wants
> To . . . hold us upside down
> And shake all the nonsense out.[3]

Joy and mercy.

These are two things that are promised in the Old Testament to come each morning. This causes me to think though, that the writers Jeremiah and David knew that on a daily basis we must need these because our hearts would be broken, disheartened and with sorrow. We are in need of the daily dose of joy and mercy.

Some people live for the mornings, they cannot wait to wake up. Others consider themselves the owls of creation and just start getting into their groove as other people are going to bed. Then there are those who require an ample amount of sleep and then they can conquer the world.

No matter what the preference, each of us needs to go to bed. And we need to wake up. I still fall asleep with questions, ever-growing in their complexity, yet the wrestling is honest. It is holy. It is gut-wrenching, and tear-stained pillows are real at times; yet God is the one who sees us. In the darkness of silent nights or when all seems well, God sees us! I continue to choose to stay with my questions, to voice them out loud at times with a trusted person, as well as to stay with others in theirs. It is hard to feel alone in areas of complexity surrounding our longing to connect, to belong, and to be known; but being transparent about what one does not know requires courage, as in Latin the word "courage" means "to offer from your whole heart."

Be courageous!

---

3. Hafiz, *Gift*, 187.

God sees you and hears you even when you cannot comprehend.

Hold on fiercely to these words, be alive in freedom, present to mercy, and full of joy!

Your desire for longing and belonging will feel complicated and mysterious at times. Be kind and compassionate to yourself as you ask the questions from the depths of what you do not yet understand. May you stay awake late into the night with your unedited slew of questions. The Divine is listening. And then tomorrow when it is time for you to wake up, may there be an awareness of the Triune God's love.

Love comes in the early-morning greetings of joy and mercy and is present throughout the day into the evening. There is longing to experience meaning in the world propelling people to explore the essence of belonging. As Jesus followers continue to pursue the abundant life that John 10:10 describes, there will come a day when the chaos of earth will experience full restoration: the kingdom of heaven will be ready to feast around a table together.

Until that day comes, there is an ongoing invitation for movement toward oneness with the Triune God, while still living at peace along with mercy in the process until that day comes. In the final scene in the Chronicles of Narnia, C. S. Lewis portrays the end of the story as people know it here on earth, while the one of eternity is about to begin:

> And as He spoke, He no longer looked to them like a lion; but the things that began to happen after that were so great and beautiful that I cannot write them. And for us this the end of all the stories, and we can most truly say that they all lived happily ever after. But for them it was only the beginning of the real story. All their life in this world and all their adventures in Narnia had only been the cover and the title page: now at last they were beginning Chapter One of the Great Story which no one on earth has read: which goes on forever: in which every chapter is better than the one before.[4]

4. Lewis, *Last Battle*, 72.

Bibliography

Adamson, Dave. "Photo of an Open Bible by Dave Adamson." *Instagram*, April 15, 2020. https://www.instagram.com/p/B-_2nMCHH74/.

Alexander, Christopher. "Making the Garden." *First Things*, February 2016. https://www.firstthings.com/article/2016/02/making-the-garden.

Altmann, Peter, and Janling Fu. *Feasting in the Archaeology and Texts of the Bible and the Ancient Near East*. Winona Lake, IN: Eisenbrauns, 2014.

Ayres, Jennifer. *Good Food: Grounded Practical Theology*. Waco, TX: Baylor University Press, 2013.

Berry, Wendell. *The Mad Farmer Poems*. Large-print ed. Canada: Accessible Publishing, 2010.

Böckmann, Aquinata. *Around the Monastic Table—RB 31–42: Growing in Mutual Service and Love*. Edited by Marianne Burkhard. Collegeville, MN: Liturgical, 2009.

Bonhoeffer, Dietrich. *Life Together: A Discussion of Christian Fellowship*. San Francisco, CA: HarperOne, 1954.

Boyce, Geoff. *An Improbable Feast: The Surprising Dynamic of Hospitality at the Heart of Multifaith Chaplaincy*. Glandore, South Australia: Boyce, 2010.

Brasher-Cunningham, Milton. *Keeping the Feast: Metaphors for the Meal*. Harrisburg: Morehouse, 2012.

Braun, Adee. "Alone Together: The Return of Communal Restaurant Tables." *The Atlantic*, March 31, 2014. http://www.theatlantic.com/health/archive/2014/03/alone-together-the-return-of-communal-restaurant-tables/284481/.

Brown, Brené. *I Thought It Was Just Me (But It Isn't): Making the Journey from "What Will People Say," to "I Am Enough."* New York: Avery, 2007.

———. *Rising Strong: The Reckoning. The Rumble. The Revolution*. New York: Spiegel & Grau, 2015.

Chapell, Bryan. *Christ-Centered Worship: Letting the Gospel Shape Our Practice*. Grand Rapids, MI: Baker, 2009.

Cherry, Constance. *The Worship Architect: The Blueprint for Designing Culturally Relevant and Biblically Faithful Services*. Grand Rapids, MI: Baker Academic, 2010.

Chester, Tim. *A Meal with Jesus: Discovering Grace, Community, and Mission Around the Table*. Wheaton, IL: Crossway, 2011.

Christian Reformed Church. "7–12 Creation." https://www.crcna.org/welcome/beliefs/our-world-belongs-god/7-12-creation.

Chu, Jeff. "Photo of Soil in Planter by Jeff Chu." *Instagram*, March 24, 2020. https://www.instagram.com/p/B-Hiq7yhPnJ/.

"Church Attendance Trends Around the Country." https://www.barna.com/research/church-attendance-trends-around-country/.

Clapp, Steve, and Fred Bernhard. *Hospitality: Life Without Fear*. The Lifequest Growing in Faith Series. Fort Wayne, IN: LifeQuest, 2000.

"Communication." https://www.dictionary.com/browse/communication.

David, Susan. *Emotional Agility: Get Unstuck, Embrace Change, and Thrive in Work and Life*. New York: Avery, 2016.

Delistraty, Cody C. "The Importance of Eating Together." *The Atlantic*, July 18, 2014. https://www.theatlantic.com/health/archive/2014/07/the-importance-of-eating-together/374256/.

Diamant, Anita, and Howard Cooper. *Living a Jewish Life: Jewish Traditions, Customs, and Values for Today's Families*. Rev. ed. New York: HarperCollins, 2007.

Diamant, Anita, and Karen Kushner. *How to Raise a Jewish Child: A Practical Handbook for Family Life*. Reprint ed. New York: Schocken, 2008.

Eldredge, John. *Waking the Dead: The Glory of a Heart Fully Alive*. Nashville: Nelson, 2006.

"Eucharist." http://www.dictionary.com/browse/eucharist.

Evans, Rachel Held. *Searching for Sunday: Loving, Leaving, and Finding the Church*. Grand Rapids, MI: Nelson, 2015.

Fick, Gary W. *Food, Farming, and Faith*. Albany, NY: State University of New York Press, 2008.

Fieldhouse, Paul. "Eating Together: The Culture of the Family Meal." https://vanierinstitute.ca/eating-culture-family-meal/.

Flynn, Thomas. *Existentialism: A Very Short Introduction*. New York: Oxford University Press, 2006.

Fowler, Jeaneane, et al. *World Religions: An Introduction for Students*. Rev. ed. Portland, OR: Sussex Academic, 1997.

Fresco, Louise O. "Why We Eat Together." *The Atlantic*, November 26, 2015. http://www.louiseofresco.com/pdf/UK_Publications/20151126_The_Atlantic_Louise_O_Fresco_Eating_Dinner_Together.pdf.

Garrels, Josh. "At the Table." Track 10 on *Home*. Small Voice Records, 2015. https://joshgarrels.bandcamp.com/track/at-the-table.

Gottschall, Jonathan. *The Storytelling Animal: How Stories Make Us Human*. New York: Mariner, 2013.

Gray, Mel, et al., eds. *Indigenous Social Work Around the World: Towards Culturally Relevant Education and Practice*. Aldershot: Ashgate, 2008.

Groppe, Elizabeth T. *Eating and Drinking*. Minneapolis: Fortress, 2011.

Haas, J. Craig. *Readings from Mennonite Writings, New and Old*. Intercourse, PA: Good Books, 1992.

Bibliography

Hafiz. *The Gift: Poems by Hafiz, the Great Sufi Master.* Translated by Daniel Ladínsky. Penguin, 1999.

Hamaker, Sarah. "Pew for One: How Is the Church Responding to Growing Number of Singles?" *The Christian Post*, February 29, 2012. http://www. christianpost.com/news/pew-for-one-how-is-the-church-responding-to-growing-number-of-singles-70586/.

Harper, Lisa Sharon. *The Very Good Gospel: How Everything Wrong Can Be Made Right.* Colorado Springs: Waterbrook, 2016.

Hellerman, Joseph H. *When the Church Was a Family: Recapturing Jesus' Vision for Authentic Christian Community.* Nashville: B&H Academic, 2009.

Hershberger, Michele. *A Christian View of Hospitality: Expecting Surprises.* Scottdale, PA: Herald, 1999.

Heschel, Abraham Joshua. *Moral Grandeur and Spiritual Audacity: Essays.* United States: Farrar, Straus & Giroux, 1997.

Heuertz, Christopher L. *The Enneagram of Belonging: A Compassionate Journey of Self-Acceptance.* United States: Zondervan, 2020.

Hicks, John Mark. *Come to the Table: Revisioning the Lord's Supper.* Abilene, TX: Leafwood, 2008.

Hirsch, Debra. *Redeeming Sex: Naked Conversations About Sexuality and Spirituality.* Downers Grove, IL: InterVarsity, 2015.

"Invitation." https://www.dictionary.com/browse/invitation.

James, Aaron. *Assholes: A Theory.* Reprint. New York: Anchor, 2014.

Julier, Alice P. *Eating Together: Food, Friendship and Inequality.* Champaigne, IL: University of Illinois Press, 2013.

Jung, L. Shannon. *Food for Life: The Spirituality and Ethics of Eating.* Minneapolis: Augsburg Fortress, 2004.

Klaver, Brad. "Photo of A Leaf by Brad Klaver." Instagram, April 9, 2020. https://www.instagram.com/p/B-wsvG4Do6qWuJX8qgB52bQO2WPfm 3Ly7cKXQUo/

Kurosaki, Kokichi. *One Body in Christ.* Northridge, CA: Voice Christian, 1968.

Ladd, George E. *The Young Church: Acts of the Apostles.* Bible Guides 15. Nashville: Abingdon, 1964.

LaVerdiere, Eugene. *Dining in the Kingdom of God: The Origins of the Eucharist According to Luke.* Chicago, IL: Liturgy Training, 2007.

Leithart, Peter. *Blessed Are the Hungry: Meditation on the Lord's Supper.* Moscow, ID: Canon, 2000.

Lemons, J. Derrick. "Communities at the Tables: Jesus, the Marginalized, and the Modern Church." *The Asbury Journal* 70.1 (2015) 157–70.

Lewis, C. S. *The Last Battle.* Reprint ed. New York: HarperCollins, 2002.

———. *The Weight of Glory and Other Addresses.* San Francisco: HarperOne, 2001.

Lischer, Richard A. *Theology of Preaching: The Dynamics of the Gospel.* Eugene, OR: Wipf & Stock, 1992.

MacDonald, Nathan. *What Did the Ancient Israelites Eat? Diet in Biblical Times.* Grand Rapids, MI: Eerdmans, 2008.

Bibliography

MacDonald, Nathan, et al., eds. *Decisive Meals: Table Politics in Biblical Literature.* New York: T. & T. Clark, 2014.

McClay, Wilfred M., and Ted V. McAllister, eds. *Why Place Matters: Geography, Identity, and Civic Life in Modern America.* New York: Encounter, 2014.

McElvaney, William K. *Eating and Drinking at the Welcome Table: The Holy Supper for All People.* St. Louis: Chalice, 1998.

McMinn, Lisa Graham. *The Contented Soul: The Art of Savoring Life.* Downers Grove, IL: InterVarsity, 2006.

———. *To the Table: A Spirituality of Food, Farming, and Community.* Grand Rapids, MI: Brazos, 2016.

McMinn, Lisa Graham, and Megan Anna Neff. *Walking Gently on the Earth: Making Faithful Choices About Food, Energy, Shelter and More.* Downers Grove, IL: InterVarsity, 2010.

Menakem, Resmaa. *My Grandmother's Hands: Racialized Trauma and the Pathway to Mending Our Hearts and Bodies.* Las Vegas: Central Recovery, 2017.

Milne, Bruce. *We Belong Together: The Meaning of Fellowship.* Downers Grove, IL: InterVarsity, 1978.

Minich, Deanna M. *The Rainbow Diet: A Holistic Approach to Radiant Health through Foods and Supplements.* Newbuyerport, MA: Conari, 2018.

Moser, Drew. *The Enneagram of Discernment.* Beaver Falls PA: Falls City Press, 2020.

Nouwen, Henri J. M. *Bread for the Journey: A Daybook of Wisdom and Faith.* New York: HarperCollins, 1997.

———. *Creative Ministry.* New York: Doubleday, 1971.

———. *Eternal Seasons: A Spiritual Journey through the Church's Year.* Edited by Michael Ford. Notre Dame, IN: Ave Maria, 2007.

———. *Show Me the Way: Readings for Each Day of Lent.* New York: Crossroad, 1992.

O'Donohue, John. *To Bless the Space between Us: A Book of Blessings.* New York: Doubleday, 2008.

Parker, Priya. *Art of Gathering: How We Meet and Why It Matters.* New York: Riverhead, 2020.

"Participation." https://www.dictionary.com/browse/participation.

Pastor, Paul J. *The Listening Day: Meditations on the Way.* Vol. 1. Portland, OR: Zeal, 2017.

Perel, Esther. *Mating in Captivity: Reconciling the Erotic and the Domestic.* New York: HaperCollins, 2006.

Pohl, Christine D. *Living into Community: Cultivating Practices That Sustain Us.* Grand Rapids, MI: Eerdmans, 2011.

———. *Making Room: Recovering Hospitality as a Christian Tradition.* Grand Rapids, MI: Eerdmans, 1999.

Pointer Adams, Julie. *Wabi-Sabi Welcome: Learning to Embrace the Imperfect and Entertain with Thoughtfulness and Ease.* New York: Artisan, 2017.

Pollan, Michael. *Cooked: A Natural History of Transformation.* New York: Penguin, 2014.

Redekop, Calvin. *Mennonite Society*. Baltimore: Johns Hopkins University Press, 1989.

Roberts McWilliams, Susan. "Love, Loss and Fruit Salad." *Cooking Light*, October 2015.

Rohr, Richard. *Divine Dance: The Trinity and Your Transformation*. New Kensington, PA: Whitaker, 2016.

———. "Mysticism: Week 2: Julian of Norwich, Part I." https://cac.org/julian-norwich-part-1-2017-10-01/.

Scazzero, Peter. *Emotionally Healthy Spirituality*. Updated ed. Nashville: Integrity, 2017.

Schell, Kristin. *The Turquoise Table: Finding Community and Connection in Your Own Front Yard*. Nashville: Nelson, 2017.

Schultz, Howard, and Joanne Gordon. *Onward: How Starbucks Fought for Its Life Without Losing Its Soul*. Reprint ed. New York: Rodale, 2012.

Siegel, Daniel J., and Tina Payne Bryson. *The Whole-Brain Child: 12 Revolutionary Strategies to Nurture Your Child's Developing Mind*. New York: Bantam, 2012.

Smith, Dennis E., and Hal Taussig, eds. *Meals in the Early Christian World: Social Formation, Experimentation and Conflict at the Table*. London: Palgrave Macmillan, 2012.

Smith, Gordon T. *A Holy Meal: The Lord's Supper in the Life of the Church*. Grand Rapids, MI: Baker Academic, 2005.

Steel, Carolyn. *Hungry City: How Food Shapes Our Lives*. Reprint ed. London: Random House, 2013.

Stewart, Don. "What Was the Significance of Jesus' Transfiguration?" https://www.blueletterbible.org/faq/don_stewart/don_stewart_786.cfm.

Stookey, Laurence Hull. *Eucharist: Christ's Feast with the Church*. Nashville: Abingdon, 1993.

Strickland, Cara. "Hospitality by the Pint." *Living Lutheran* (blog), September 11, 2017. https://www.livinglutheran.org/2017/09/hospitality%E2%80%85by-the-pint/.

Strong, James. *The New Strong's Expanded Exhaustive Concordance of the Bible*. Nashville, Tennessee: Nelson, 2001.

Sweet, Leonard. *The Bad Habits of Jesus: Showing Us the Way to Live Right in a World Gone Wrong*. Carol Stream, IL: Tyndale House, 2016.

———. *From Tablet to Table: Where Community is Found and Identity Is Formed*. Colorado Springs: NavPress, 2015.

———. *The Gospel According to Starbucks: Living with a Grande Passion*. Colorado Springs: WaterBrook, 2007.

———. *Mother Tongue: How Our Heritage Shapes Our Legacy*. Colorado Springs: NavPress, 2017.

———. *Nudge: Awakening Each Other to the God Who's Already There*. Colorado Springs: Cook, 2010.

Sweet, Leonard, and Frank Viola. *Jesus Speaks: Learning to Recognize and Respond to the Lord's Voice*. Nashville: Nelson, 2016.

Bibliography

Taussig, Hal. *In the Beginning was the Meal: Social Experimentation and Early Christian Identity*. Minneapolis: Fortress, 2009.

Taylor, Barbara Brown. *An Altar in the World: A Geography of Faith*. Reprint ed. New York: HarperOne, 2010.

Tippett, Krista. "Listening as an Act of Love." *On Being* (podcast), May 12, 2016. https://onbeing.org/programs/david-isay-listening-as-an-act-of-love/.

Tuama, Pádraig Ó. *In the Shelter: Finding a Home in the World*. London: Hodder, 2016.

Tutu, Desmond, and Mpho Tutu. *The Book of Forgiving: The Fourfold Path for Healing Ourselves and Our World*. Reprint ed. New York: HarperOne, 2014.

"Unification." https://www.dictionary.com/browse/unification.

Van der Kolk, Bessel A. *The Body Keeps the Score: Brain, Mind, and Body in the Healing of Trauma*. New York: Penguin, 2015.

Vander Zee, Leonard. *Christ, Baptism, and the Lord's Supper: Recovering the Sacraments for Evangelical Worship*. Downers Grove, IL: IVP Academic, 2004.

Vermilya, Emily. "This Is the Feast: Experiencing the Full Spectrum of God's Story at the Table." *Seedbed: New Room* (blog), November 24, 2016. http://www.seedbed.com/this-is-the-feast-experiencing-the-full-spectrum-of-gods-story-at-the-table/.

Warren, Kay. *Choose Joy Devotional: Finding Joy No Matter What You're Going Through*. Grand Rapids, MI: Revell, 2015.

Webster, Douglas. *Table Grace: The Role of Hospitality in the Christian Life*. Scotland: Christian Focus, 2001.

Weil, Simone. *Waiting for God*. Minneapolis: Harper, 2009.

Welker, Michael. *What Happens in Holy Communion?* Grand Rapids, MI: Eerdmans, 2000.

Willimon, William H. *Sunday Dinner: The Lord's Supper and the Christian Life*. Nashville: Upper Room, 1998.

Willis, Dustin, and Brandon Clements. *The Simplest Way to Change the World: Biblical Hospitality as a Way of Life*. Chicago, IL: Moody, 2017.

Wood, Julia T. *Interpersonal Communication: Everyday Encounters*. 8th ed. Boston, MA: Wadsworth, 2015.

"Xenia the Ancient Greek Concept of Hospitality." http://www.sfakia-xenia-hotel.gr/en/ancient.

Zizioulas, John D. *Being as Communion: Studies in Personhood and the Church*. Crestwood, NY: St. Vladimirs Seminary Press, 1997.